journey to freedom

finding release from spiritual bondage
a study of Exodus 1-18

Jill McSheehy

Copywright 2018 by Jill McSheehy

All rights reserved. No part of this book may be reproduced in any form without permission in writing by the author, except in the case of brief quotations with appropriate reference.

Scriptures taken from the Holy Bible, Christian Standard Bible, Copyright 2017 by Holman Bible Publishers

Edited by Deborah Lynn Howard
Cover Design: Jill McSheehy

acknowledgments

I'm deeply grateful to my senior pastor, Greg Sykes, and equipping pastor, Michael Cloud, of First Baptist Church Russellville, Arkansas, for reading over and critiquing this manuscript. Your insights, support, and encouraging words were invaluable. In this and in every area of your leadership, you are a living example of Ephesians 4:12. Thank you.

meet jill

Jill McSheehy is the wife to Matt and mom to Drew and Alyssa. She enjoys gardening, reading, and relaxing with her daily cappuccino.

After obtaining her Bachelor's Degree in psychology from Arkansas Tech University, Jill spent a decade in management at a local Ford dealership. When her son was 6 and her daughter 2, she left her job to become a stay-at-home mom. Now that her kids are in school, Jill spends her time writing, podcasting, teaching people how to garden, and writing Bible studies -- her lifelong dream.

Connect with Jill on her web site at journeywithjill.net.

contents

Introduction..................6
Week 1......................9
Week 2....................39
Week 3....................67
Week 4....................91
Week 5....................115
Week 6....................139

introduction

Freedom.

What comes to mind when you hear it? Maybe you think of America, carefree living, or escape from bondage. Whatever your picture of freedom is, most likely it's good, refreshing, and desirable.

We want freedom, right? But how do we know if we have it?

Could it be -- in our hearts and in our lives -- we are walking enslaved to a master we can't identify? Perhaps we're even unaware of our enslavement!

It was true of me (and still is true at times). Warning signs blared in my life -- dissatisfaction, broken relationships, insecurity -- but I had no idea from where these issues originated.

I limped through life, unaware of the chains I dragged along with each faltering step. Some chains came from deep in my past. Some I picked up along the way.

For freedom Christ has set you free. It's a nice thought, isn't it? And many of us know it's a promise from Scripture. What does freedom in Christ look like? And how do we live in it?

I began my quest to discover these answers by reading in the book of Exodus. I didn't plan to write a Bible study, but the truths I found in the first eighteen chapters were too incredible not to share with a fellow sojourner.

What I found in these pages transcended the nation of Israel and story of Moses -- though the story itself is pretty amazing. And admittedly, because I like this kind of thing, I immersed myself in the historical background that in many ways brought this story to life.

Most importantly, though an Old Testament book, I found Jesus all over its pages, drawing us pictures of Himself. And of us.

As you dig into this study and into your own copy of Exodus, immerse yourself in the story. Let it seep deeply into your soul.

But prepare to do some hard soul-searching, too. We can't have freedom without coming face to face with our captor, and what I learned is that sometimes my captor is me.

My hope is that by the time you reach the final day of this study, you will find yourself on your own journey to freedom as you leave your chains behind.

It's not an easy journey, but it's worth it.

Jill

Study Tools:

historical background
To understand the fullness of a text, many times it's helpful to know what was going on in history at the time. Don't worry; even non-history buffs will find these tidbits fascinating and helpful.

in context
In order to understand what Scripture is saying to us, we must first understand what it said to its original audience. "In context" will help broaden your view with the verses surrounding the text as well as the entire Bible's message.

Christ in exodus
More than a book about Moses or even about freedom, Exodus is a book about Jesus Christ and the freedom He would ultimately provide. In this section you'll see hints of Christ Himself and His future work.

cross-reference
A central rule of Bible study is "let Scripture interpret Scripture." I'll provide cross-references that help broaden your understanding of the text.

dig deeper
The Bible is like an endless gold mine. None of us will ever reach the end of its depths, but through "Dig Deeper," I'll lead you to think a little more deeply.

definition
If the text contains an unclear term, I'll define it for you.

interesting facts
Though not central to each day's study, "interesting facts" can help you understand the broader context and in many cases expand your knowledge on the cultural issues at play.

symbols & types
Just as we see Christ in Exodus, we can also see multiple symbols and "types" that point to Christ, salvation, and the full work of the gospel as fulfilled in the New Testament.

further application
Though most of the commentary portion will remain objective, provoking questions will prod you to an application of the text in addition to the devotional application for each day.

> For freedom, christ set us free. stand firm then and don't submit again to a yoke of slavery.
>
> Galatians 5:1

Week 1 Day 1

Exodus 1:1-14

Observations ~ Main Points ~ Questions ~ Application:

....

....

....

....

....

....

HISTORICAL BACKGROUND

Though historical and biblical scholars are not certain, evidence suggests that Joseph rose to power when the Hyksos ruled Egypt. A Semitic people, the Hyksos, like the Hebrews, descended from Noah's son, Shem, and more specifically, Abraham. By the time of our text today, the native Egyptians had ousted the Hyksos and reclaimed power. Because the Hebrews shared their Semitic roots with the Hyksos, this might account for Pharaoh's distrust of the Hebrew people, though no evidence shows them to have ever been a threat to Egypt to this point.

definition

Rameses: the city in Goshen where the Israelites lived since Joseph's time (Gen. 47:11).
Pithom: 20 miles south of Rameses.

CROSS-REFERENCE

In Genesis 46:3 (in the margin), what promise did God make to the Israelite nation?

....

....

"God said, 'I am God, the God of your father. Do not be afraid to go down to Egypt, for I will make you into a great nation there.'" (Genesis 46:3)

He took five of his brothers and presented them to Pharaoh. And Pharaoh asked his brothers, "What is your occupation?"

They said to Pharaoh, "Your servants, both we and our fathers, are shepherds." And they said to Pharaoh, "We have come to stay in the land for a while because there is no grazing land for your servants' sheep, since the famine in the land of Canaan has been severe. So now, please let your servants settle in the land of Goshen."

Then Pharaoh said to Joseph, "Now that your father and brothers have come to you, the land of Egypt is open before you; settle your father and brothers in the best part of the land. They can live in the land of Goshen. If you know of any capable men among them, put them in charge of my livestock." (Genesis 47:2-6)

CROSS-REFERENCE

Read Genesis 47:2-6 in the margin.

What was the Israelites' native occupation, which they continued in Egypt?

....

In contrast, in Exodus 1:14, what was their current job?

....

Brick-making was a filthy, muddy job in those days. The tasks entailed fetching straw, breaking it up, hauling mud and water, shaping bricks, setting bricks to dry, and hauling them on site. Bricks for large buildings could have been as large as 12" by 6" by 6". Think of the size of a cinderblock.

interesting fact

One study calculated that for the Israelites to have increased from seventy coming into Egypt to approximately two million at the exodus, each family would have had to have an average of eight children during those four hundred years.

DIG DEEPER

List five descriptors of the Hebrew people in Egypt and note the progression. With seventy people arriving in Egypt, the estimated total number of people leaving Egypt would inflate to around two million.

- ....

- ....

- ....

- ....

- ....

fear as a slave driver

My feet pounded the pavement as I considered three specific situations with which I was struggling -- anger toward my children, conflict with my husband, and bitterness in a situation where something didn't go as I had hoped.

My thoughts floated to the Exodus text I had just read that morning. In a way, I had to admit, I felt enslaved by these situations. Seeking to discover guidance from the text, I asked myself, why did Pharaoh decide to oppress and enslave the Israelite people?

The answer leapt from my memory. Fear. It all came down to fear. For reasons we can only speculate, Pharaoh feared the Israelites would seek to overthrow his power.

> **symbols & types**
> Egypt represents the world system. It opposes God's people and seeks to keep them in bondage.

Could that be my problem as well? Could fear be the driving force behind these areas in my life I couldn't seem to overcome?

One by one, I analyzed these situations at the root of my anxiety. One by one, I traced the root to fear.

Anger toward my children could be traced back to the fear of how they would turn out if they continued behaving a certain way. Or, if I'm honest, I feared what others would think about my parenting if they saw these behaviors in public.

> The enemy's tactics are the same today as then: Keep the people enslaved, and they can't or won't join God. This can apply to both believers in Christ and unbelievers.

A resistance to humbly submit to my husband was rooted in my fear that he might make a decision I disagreed with.

A specific bitterness was, at its root, a fear of a situation not working out the way I wanted it to.

I realized that day that fear, as a driving force, always leads to slavery.

Maybe that's why the Bible repeats the message, "Do not be afraid" over and over. We cannot be wholehearted servants of God and slaves to fear at the same time.

application

Think about recent situations causing you anxiety. Can you trace any of them to fear? Write them out:

Situation/anxiety:

....

Fear:

....

....

Situation/anxiety:

....

Fear:

....

....

Situation/anxiety:

....

Fear:

....

....

Situation/anxiety:

....

Fear:

....

....

Go to God and confess your fear as the slave driver it is. Turn those situations over to Him, and continue giving them to Him as you seek to walk in freedom.

prayer ~ reflection ~ gratitude

to-do today

Week 1 Day 2
Exodus 1:15-22

Observations ~ Main Points ~ Questions ~ Application:

....

....

....

....

....

....

HISTORICAL BACKGROUND

By killing the infant Hebrew boys, Israel would lose their fighting men within a couple of decades. Perhaps the Egyptians thought that eventually, all the Jewish men would disappear, at which time, the Hebrew women would serve as concubines or slave girls. This male infanticide, then, began an annihilation process of the entire nation of Israel—that is, without God's intervention.

CHRIST IN EXODUS

Read the circumstances surrounding the birth of Jesus in Matthew 2:16-18 in the margin. Surrounding both Moses' and Jesus' births, the ruling kings ordered massacres of infant boys. In the midst of this terror, God providentially protected both Moses and Jesus for a higher purpose. As we will see in numerous examples throughout this study, we can observe striking parallels between Moses and Christ. Indeed, Moses himself, along with his role in bringing Israel out of slavery, paints for us a vivid picture of Jesus and how He brings us out of slavery to sin.

Then Herod, when he realized that he had been outwitted by the wise men, flew into a rage. He gave orders to massacre all the boys in and around Bethlehem who were two years old and under, in keeping with the time he had learned from the wise men. Then what was spoken through Jeremiah the prophet was fulfilled:

A voice was heard in Ramah, weeping, and great mourning, Rachel weeping for her children; and she refused to be consoled, because they are no more. (Matthew 2:16-18)

CROSS-REFERENCE

Although Scripture admonishes us to respect authorities (Romans 13:1-7), we also, in cases when God's commands oppose an earthly authority's commands, are to "obey God rather than men" (Acts 4:19, 5:29), as the midwives did here.

DIG DEEPER

The Israelites didn't find themselves in mere physical enslavement. They also faced:

- Political slavery (no voice, perceived as threats)
- Economic slavery (forced to do slave labor)
- Social slavery (not viewed as equals, treated as inferior)
- Spiritual slavery (unable to stop and worship God when they were lugging mud seven days per week)

DIG DEEPER

Scholars speculate on the true response of the midwives to Pharaoh's order. Did they lie to Pharaoh? Or, as might seem more believable, did they simply delay in getting to the laboring women?

> "Immediate blessing effected a negative action that later precipitated a larger future blessing."
> (Walvoord & Zuck, the Bible Knowledge Commentary)

Spiritual Freedom within Circumstantial Bondage

Jennifer, a friend from my youth, works with inmates in a women's prison. I remember talking with her one day about her ministry, and she told me about a woman serving a life sentence. This woman had come to know Jesus in prison, and despite no hope of release, she is one of the most joyful, Christ-filled women Jennifer knows.

This inmate's story brings to mind the midwives in today's text and the inner freedom they found despite their circumstances.

Oppressed by the government, the midwives found themselves in bondage to a cruel tyrant who ordered the drowning of baby boys. But these midwives -- whom Moses respected enough to pen their names when he wrote Exodus -- feared God, though they had no promise of freedom during their lifetimes.

> Obedience to God doesn't mean terror will not come. But in the midst of terror, God blessed the midwives for their brave obedience. Is God asking you for brave obedience in the midst of a difficult situation?

In fact, since Moses would not lead the Israelites out of Egypt for another eighty years, it's unlikely Shiphrah and Puah even lived to see freedom.

Though they lived in physical bondage, I can't help but think they lived in freedom where it mattered—within their hearts.

It is possible to fear God and devote ourselves to Him while still living in physical bondage of one kind or another. It could be prison, like Jennifer's friend. Or it could be a job you hate. Or a rocky marriage. Or a debilitating disease.

True freedom, you see, isn't tied to our outward circumstances. If we live our lives thinking we could be free if only this or that circumstance would change, we may find ourselves waiting a long time -- perhaps our entire lives.

application

What circumstances in your life might you consider constraining, limiting your freedom? List them below:

....

....

....

....

....

....

....

....

Week 1 Day 3
Exodus 2:1-10

Observations ~ Main Points ~ Questions ~ Application:

HISTORICAL BACKGROUND

As Pharaoh's daughter's adopted son, Moses received an Egyptian education. Since Egypt was a well-known and highly developed civilization at the time, most likely he received training in engineering, mathematics, astronomy, literature, arts, warfare, foreign languages, speech, and debate. Egypt also had developed an astutely accurate calendar. No doubt this knowledge came in helpful after the Exodus, when God instructed Moses to begin a new system of keeping the calendar based on the Passover.

CHRIST IN EXODUS

The basket, like Noah's ark, points ahead to Christ's saving work. (Ark and basket are the same Hebrew word.) Just like the ark saved Noah's family and the basket saved Moses, Jesus Christ shelters us from God's judgment and saves us from certain demise.

"Moses" in Egyptian means "child" or "son" or "is born." This is likely what Pharaoh's daughter had in mind when she named him. But, "Moses" in Hebrew means "drawn out," showing God's sovereignty not only in Moses' circumstances as a baby -- being drawn out of the Nile -- but also his destiny -- leading the Israelites as God drew out the people from captivity.

CROSS-REFERENCE

In Exodus 2:2, Moses' mother described him as a "beautiful child," but this sentiment went beyond a mother's affection. Compare Acts 7:20 and Hebrews 11:23 below to see how Luke and the author of Hebrews describe Moses:

> *"At this time Moses was born, and he was beautiful in God's sight. He was cared for in his father's home for three months,"* (Acts 7:20).

> *"By faith Moses, after he was born, was hidden by his parents for three months, because they saw that the child was beautiful, and they didn't fear the king's edict,"* (Hebrews 11:23).

the invisible chains of pride

I swallowed, coffee in hand, and met my best friend's patient eyes. Even though we've been friends for almost twenty years, admitting my sin didn't come easy. Though not a sin against her, this attitude of pride needed to be brought to light.

I would have preferred to deal with it on my own, naturally.

But that was the problem. Pride itself prevented me from admitting my sin, and I knew to break free, I needed to confess it with someone I trusted.

She smiled gently and nodded. My admission didn't come as a surprise to her, but for me, it was a breakthrough moment.

We don't have to be born into privilege (or adopted as a prince like Moses was), to struggle with pride. Sure, it can originate from our background, our education, our level of success, or our national identity.

But more often, pride disguises itself. While we are quick to see it in others, it masquerades in our own lives. And as long as it goes unrecognized and unchecked, we will never walk in the unfettered freedom Jesus has won for us.

application

Because pride can be difficult to recognize at times, it helps to come face to face with some of its "fruit." Then, we can get at its "root." Place a check beside any of these attributes that describe you.

___ critical of others
___ want to be right
___ desire for personal success
___ jealous of others
___ self-conscious
___ look down on others
___ reputation is a big deal
___ trouble admitting wrong
___ upset when overlooked
___ defensive when criticized
___ cover up sin
___ compare yourself with others
___ slow to let others know you
___ trouble confessing specific sin
___ confidence in personal knowledge
___ difficult to share your needs with others

If we're honest, we all nurse pride to some degree or another. It's part of our flesh -- our sinful nature. But this isn't an area God overlooks. He will not use a person with a prideful spirit, partly because it enslaves us so deeply, and partly because when we harbor pride we seek to rob Him of the glory only He deserves.

What area of pride is the easiest for you to see?

....

....

....

....

....

What is the hardest to admit?

....

....

....

....

....

Write out a confession. Don't skip this part. Admitting it outside of your head is one key step to repentance.

....

....

....

....

....

....

....

Consider the verse to the right and ask God how He would have you respond to this verse. If God is leading you to reach out to a trusted friend or confidant, write out your next step below:

....

....

....

....

"Therefore, confess your sins to one another and pray for one another, so that you may be healed," (James 5:16a).

prayer ~ reflection ~ gratitude

to-do today

Week 1 Day 4
Exodus 2:11-25

Observations ~ Main Points ~ Questions ~ Application:

HISTORICAL BACKGROUND

Conservative historians speculate that either Amenhotep I or Thutmose I reigned as Pharaoh at the time of Moses' birth. In the first forty years of Moses' life, Thutmose II reigned for a short period until his untimely death. Then, Thutmose II's wife and step-sister Hatshepsut assumed the throne until his infant son (from another wife) was old enough to reign. After her death, Thutmose III came to power, and it is likely Thutmose III wasn't as accommodating to Moses' presence as the previous leaders were. Perhaps this leadership change -- and increasing oppression of the Hebrews -- precipitated Moses' decision to go back to his people when he did (Acts 7:23).

CHRIST IN EXODUS

After Moses suffered rejection from his own people (Exodus 2:14), he fled to Midian, where he took a Gentile bride, Zipporah. Likewise, after suffering rejection from His own people, Jesus temporarily turned from Israel, where He symbolically took a Gentile bride -- the church! And like Moses returned for Israel, Jesus will return for Israel, as well.

"When he was forty years old, he decided to visit his own people, the Israelites. When he saw one of them being mistreated, he came to his rescue and avenged the oppressed man by striking down the Egyptian. He assumed his people would understand that God would give them deliverance through him, but they did not understand. The next day he showed up while they were fighting and tried to reconcile them peacefully, saying, 'Men, you are brothers. Why are you mistreating each other?'

"But the one who was mistreating his neighbor pushed Moses aside, saying: Who appointed you a ruler and a judge over us? Do you want to kill me, the same way you killed the Egyptian yesterday?

"When he heard this, Moses fled and became an exile in the land of Midian, where he became the father of two sons." (Acts 7:23-29)

definition
Midianites were the descendants of Midian, the son of Keturah, the wife of Abraham after Sarah died. Abraham had sent these sons of Keturah to the east, away from Isaac, without an inheritance (Genesis 25:1-6).

CROSS-REFERENCE

Read Acts 7:23-29 in the margin for Stephen's account of today's verses. What additional insight does this passage give you into today's reading?

....

....

....

Though we know from Hebrews 10:24-26 that Moses had pure motives for leaving Pharaoh's household and returning to his people, his actions arguably reveal an impulsive, impetuous side. By "looking this way and that" before killing the Egyptian, we can speculate he may have walked more by sight than by faith at that moment. Though he knew God had set him aside as a deliverer for Israel (Acts 7:25), in this action he appears to have acted out of step with God's timing.

CROSS-REFERENCE

Review Hebrews 11:24-26 below. What motivation did Moses have for leaving his regal Egyptian home and going to his oppressed people?

....

....

....

"By faith Moses, when he had grown up, refused to be called the son of Pharaoh's daughter and chose to suffer with the people of God rather than to enjoy the fleeting pleasure of sin. For he considered reproach for the sake of Christ to be greater wealth than the treasures of Egypt, since he was looking ahead to the reward," (Hebrews 11:24-26).

good desires gone bad

I sat in the parking lot of my very first job after college. My husband had just told me we hadn't been approved for the home loan yet because commission-based income couldn't be considered due to my lack of time on the job.

I remember praying, begging God to help us get that loan. We had found a nice, modest house, and I wanted more than anything for this home to be ours. But in the midst of my prayer, I felt conviction. Not once had I prayed, asking God's direction in this decision to upsize from our apartment. I let my desires control me and begged God to bless them.

Though we have every reason to believe Moses' motivation to help his people came from a pure heart, they did tempt him to take matters into his own hands instead of waiting for God.

interesting fact

Moses' rescue of Jethro's daughters represents the third time Moses had tried to rescue others (first, the Hebrew being beaten by the Egyptian, and second the Hebrews fighting with one another). What does this tell us about Moses' character? How do we see this as a foreshadowing of how God uses him later?

Like Moses' desires, many of our desires aren't wrong in themselves, but when we allow them to control us, we place those desires above God's plan, will, and timing. Unless we continue seeking the Lord with them, they can escalate to a place of unhealthy, idolatrous drive in our lives.

application

What are some of your strongest desires right now? List them below.

....

....

....

....

Prayerfully consider: Do any of these desires occupy an unhealthy place in your heart and mind? To help you answer that, consider these questions: Are you stepping ahead of God in these areas? Do you pray about them, or do you ignore them in your prayers, afraid God won't bless them? Below, list the desires that have taken a place of unhealthy prominence in your life.

....

....

....

....

When not placed under the authority and leadership of God and His Spirit, even good desires will enslave us. We will find ourselves serving our desires instead of serving God, which will always keep us in spiritual bondage. If God has brought any of these desires to your mind, release them to Him in prayer, trusting Him in these areas of your life.

FURTHER APPLICATION

God prepared Moses in 4 distinct ways:

(1) a godly home,
(2) a special education,
(3) a great failure, and
(4) a long delay.

What ways has God prepared you for His work, both in positive circumstances and within your own shortcomings and failures?

....
....
....
....
....
....
....
....
....
....

prayer ~ reflection ~ gratitude

to-do today

Week 1 Day 5

Exodus 3:1-25

Observations ~ Main Points ~ Questions ~ Application:

....

....

....

....

....

....

....

HISTORICAL BACKGROUND

"Outstretched" or "mighty" arm are common inscriptions found in Egyptian artifacts used to describe the power of the Pharaohs. In contrast, God made sure to point out that it was His mighty and outstretched arm that would defeat Pharaoh and Egypt.

IN CONTEXT

Twice God mentioned the final destination of Israel being a land "flowing with milk and honey." Abundant milk would indicate a land ideal for raising goats and cows. Honey could mean a presence of bees and flowers (indicating fruitful vegetation), or it could mean the syrup of a date, which suggested ample natural resources in the land. Ultimately, milk and honey signaled agricultural prosperity.

CHRIST IN EXODUS

It is generally believed by many scholars that the term "angel of the Lord" is the pre-incarnate appearance of Jesus Himself.

definition

Mount Horeb is the same word as Mount Sinai, where God would visit Moses after the Israelites' exodus and would give the Law.

CHRIST IN EXODUS

In the land of Canaan a half-century later, Israel would return to what they were doing before enslavement—working the land. This points to our final destination as believers in Christ. Christ will return us to what we were originally created for, before sin entered the world—to walk with God and enjoy His creation in freedom and joy.

CROSS-REFERENCE

Before Joshua and Israel would conquer Jericho, years later, Joshua encountered what most believe is another appearance of the pre-incarnate Christ, and similarly, He demands Joshua to take off his sandals for the same reason we see in this text.

> "The commander of the Lord's army said to Joshua, 'Remove the sandals from your feet, for the place where you are standing is holy.' And Joshua did that" (Joshua 5:15).

DIG DEEPER

God promised to do two things: (1) Rescue Israel from Egypt, and (2) Bring them to Canaan. But, as listed in verse 12, the purpose of God rescuing Israel was not only that they would find freedom, but even more so that they would worship Him.

DIG DEEPER

Even the Promised Land of freedom had enemies to be conquered. Similarly, after we've received Christ as Savior and He has brought us into spiritual freedom, we must expect to face enemies.

---

definition
The word "worship" in Hebrew (v.12) means "to serve" or "to be a slave." Thus, when God called Israel to worship Him, He called them to renounce their slavery to Egypt and instead to serve Him. It's not possible to serve two masters, (Matt. 6:24).

interesting fact
It is in this text that the word "holy" is used for the first time in the Bible.

the lie that you've ruined God's plan for your life

I gazed out the Texas hotel window at the bright sky and tender leaves on the trees. How could nature look so serene when I felt so anxious?

My husband had just been told that his company would be closing its office in Arkansas, and we had two choices: accept a layoff, or transfer to Waco, Texas. Circumstances tense at my own job, I wondered how much my bubbling desire to quit and write full-time contributed to my confusion about this major life decision.

Could a move to Texas bring me freedom from my job and clear the path to pursue the calling I felt God had placed on my heart?

Though everything within me wanted to make God's timing fit into mine, something didn't feel right. My husband declined the job, and over the next few years we were able to watch a more amazing plan unfold in our lives. This Bible study is just one of the many results.

Yet, thinking back to how tempting it was to rush God's timing, I understand Moses in his youth. He had such a heart to do the right thing, to follow God's path. When he stepped ahead of God just a bit and all his dreams and plans crashed, I can only imagine the tremendous loss he felt. Had his impulsive actions ruined God's plan?

At the beginning of chapter 3, we see that the answer is no. Moses didn't ruin God's plan. In fact, his detour into the wilderness, his Gentile wife, and even his new occupation as a shepherd pointed to Christ's future work to save humanity.

After forty years, God called him back to Himself, for a purpose greater than Moses could have ever dreamed of.

What about us and our past mistakes? Perhaps we made an impulsive decision in our youth. Perhaps we skipped ahead of God and watched our dreams burn. Do we, in our heart of hearts, believe we've messed up God's plan for our lives? Can anyone truly thwart the will of God?

Your enemy would have you believe you've ruined everything, that there are no second chances, that God can't use you now, that you may as well give up on living a godly life. But please hear me -- that's a lie!

I'm sure Moses' stay in Midian wasn't his first choice, but through those years in solitude and unassuming service as a shepherd, God humbled him and prepared him.

application

What mistakes, errors in judgment, or past sins have you been unable to get past? Write them below (generalities are fine if you're working through this in a group).

....

....

....

....

....

What would your life look like if you understood that you didn't mess up God's plan for you? What lies do you need to acknowledge and banish from your mind in order to walk in freedom from this day forward?

....

....

....

....

....

....

....

> The Lord didn't call out to Moses until he went to the bush. Does God want us to stop what we're doing and "come look" before He speaks to us?

....

....

....

....

....

....

....

prayer ~ reflection ~ gratitude

to-do today

Week 2 Day 1
Exodus 4:1-17

Observations ~ Main Points ~ Questions ~ Application:

IN CONTEXT

In the three signs God gave Moses, a twofold meaning emerges. First, God revealed His power over the Egyptian gods and ideals. But further, we see God's power over the world and His ultimate plan -- saving people from their sin.

In the first sign, God turned Moses' staff into a snake and back. In recovered Egyptian art, serpent creatures represented Pharaoh, and snakes themselves symbolized power and life to the Egyptians. The rod represented authority, showing Moses God's power over Pharaoh and Egypt. Beyond Egypt, this sign symbolized God's power over Satan and the world.

In the second sign, Moses' hand became leprous and then clean again. Considered incurable in Egypt, this skin disease represented another sign of God's power over the impossible. In other parts of Scripture, leprosy also symbolized sin, thus this sign foreshadowed God's final plan of cleansing His people from sin.

In the third sign, God told Moses to take water from the Nile and it would turn to blood. In Egypt the Nile was deified as a source of life and productivity in Egypt. This symbolized, in the short-term, God's power over the Nile and natural forces but in the long-term, it predicted that both Israel's and Christians' lives would be redeemed by blood.

CROSS-REFERENCE

Review Exodus 3:18. God had already told Moses that the people of Israel would listen to him. His response here in 4:1 indicates his progression from fear to open unbelief in what God had already pronounced.

CROSS-REFERENCE

Look at Exodus 33:12-18 (in margin). Compare Moses' conversation with God to the one today. How has Moses' view of God changed?

....

....

....

Which Moses do we most resemble? The one in Exodus 3-4, or the one in Exodus 33?

....

DIG DEEPER

Why did God placate Moses by telling him Aaron would speak for him? In future verses, Moses would later refer to his ineffective speech as "uncircumcised lips." This would be a clear change from his focus on his present inability. With this future maturity, he would understand that his issue didn't lie in his ability or inability but rather in what was in his heart.

Moses said to the Lord, "Look, you have told me, 'Lead this people up,' but you have not let me know whom you will send with me. You said, 'I know you by name, and you have also found favor with me.' Now if I have indeed found favor with you, please teach me your ways, and I will know you, so that I may find favor with you. Now consider that this nation is your people."

And he replied, "My presence will go with you, and I will give you rest."

"If your presence does not go," Moses responded to him, "don't make us go up from here. How will it be known that I and your people have found favor with you unless you go with us? I and your people will be distinguished by this from all the other people on the face of the earth."

The Lord answered Moses, "I will do this very thing you have asked, for you have found favor with me, and I know you by name."

Then Moses said, "Please, let me see your glory." (Exodus 33:12-18)

how God responds to our insecurities

Have you ever had an itch on your back, and asked a loved one to scratch it, but they never could get to the exact spot? Frustrating, isn't it? But if they finally get there....ahhh! It makes all the difference.

I've felt that way often about how we, as Christian women, discuss our identity in Christ.

"I am loved. I am valued. I am worthy. I am special. I am chosen."

Those phrases -- all true, I might add -- seemed to always scratch right around my deepest itch but never could quite alleviate it. The conversation God has with Moses in chapters 3 and 4 of Exodus seems to lend some insight why.

When Moses objected to God's calling with questions of identity or lack of ability, God didn't respond with, "But you are loved. You are valued. You are worthy. You are special. You are chosen."

Although we know all of those things were true of Moses -- as they are of each of us -- those things weren't what Moses needed to hear. Moses needed to lose himself in God. Moses needed his sights pointed away from himself and up to the One who would do everything He said He would do. You see, it's not about us. It's all about Him.

symbols & types

Moses represents Christ, God's prophet, tasked with bringing people out of bondage by the power of God into freedom.

In future chapters we're going to see how God worked through Moses in a way that was unparalleled until Christ Himself came. Later in Exodus, beyond the reading in this study, we can watch God communicate directly with Moses like a man talks with a friend. But none of that could have happened until Moses, for lack of a better term, "got over himself."

application

In what areas of your life do you struggle with insecurity or lack of confidence?

....

....

....

....

What can you learn from God's response to Moses?

....

....

....

....

Freedom comes on the other side of ourselves. The next time you're tempted to doubt yourself and your abilities, look to God, the One who made you. He works in you in a way you could have never done on your own.

FURTHER APPLICATION

Moses was likely trained in speech and rhetoric while in Egypt. In the New Testament Stephen, in Acts 7:22, described Moses as "powerful in speech." So why would Moses say he lacked speaking ability (v. 10)?

Could it be after the events driving him from Egypt and his exile in Midian for 40 years, he lost confidence in himself?

Perhaps. But notice how God did not respond. He didn't assure Moses of his education, or of his previous ability, or even that He created Moses with a special gifting. Instead, Moses was directed back to God Himself. Moses was reminded that it was God who would provide the power, the message, and the means.

List areas in your life where you were once confident, but now you're not:

....
....
....

What has changed? Why don't you have the same confidence now?

....
....
....
....
....
....

Instead of viewing this change in yourself as loss, consider it gain. Like with Moses, God wants us to understand that He is the source of any good that comes from our words and our efforts. God needed to break down Moses' confidence in himself to make him a humble vessel through which He would work. It was not the greatness of Moses to be displayed, but the greatness of God!

Next, take those areas of insecurity you listed above, and write down how you think God would respond to these based on His response to Moses. (Use God's words in 4:11-12 as your guide.)

....

....

....

prayer ~ reflection ~ gratitude

to-do today

Week 2 Day 2
Exodus 4:18-31

Observations ~ Main Points ~ Questions ~ Application:

HISTORICAL BACKGROUND

The language God commanded Moses to use with Pharaoh in verse 22-23 held significance that Pharaoh wouldn't miss. First, "this is what the Lord says" used language a king would use with a subject. Pharaoh was looked upon as not only the king but as a god. Therefore, the use of this language pronounces God's rule over Egypt and Pharaoh -- something Pharaoh would not have taken lightly.

Second, by calling Israel His "firstborn son," God exercised His authority over His people, a people whom Pharaoh considered his subjects.

IN CONTEXT

The words translated multiple times as "harden" in the book of Exodus actually came from three different Hebrew words. The word God used to describe Pharaoh in verse 21 can mean "to strengthen." In this context, the word "harden" indicated the obstinacy of Pharaoh and alluded to God's judgment over the rebellion already present in Pharaoh's heart.

This is my covenant between me and you and your offspring after you, which you are to keep: Every one of your males must be circumcised. You must circumcise the flesh of your foreskin to serve as a sign of the covenant between me and you. Throughout your generations, every male among you is to be circumcised at eight days old—every male born in your household or purchased from any foreigner and not your offspring. Whether born in your household or purchased, he must be circumcised. My covenant will be marked in your flesh as a permanent covenant. If any male is not circumcised in the flesh of his foreskin, that man will be cut off from his people; he has broken my covenant." (Genesis 17:10-14)

Read Romans 9:14-23 for further discussion on the ways of God that do not make complete sense to us -- particularly in how and why God hardened Pharaoh's heart.

HISTORICAL BACKGROUND

In ancient Egypt, the Egyptian boys were circumcised when they turned 14 as a celebration of coming into manhood. By contrast, infant circumcision in Israel was a reminder of God's covenant with His people to the parents. Similar to today's act of baby dedications, by circumcising their infant sons, parents committed their sons to God in response to His covenant with them.

CROSS-REFERENCE

Read Genesis 17:10-14 in the margin. God required circumcision as a sign of the covenant between himself and Israel. It is unknown why Moses failed to circumcise at least one of his sons, but clearly the Lord would not let Moses go any further in this disobedience.

DIG DEEPER

In the confrontations between Pharaoh and Moses, God predicted that Pharaoh's heart would be hard and unrepentant (4:21, 7:3). Several times in future passages, the book of Exodus tells us that Pharaoh hardened his own heart (7:13-14, 22; 8:15, 19, 32; 9:7), but we also see that God Himself hardened Pharaoh's heart (9:12; 10:1, 20, 27; 11:10; 14:4,8). Notice God did not seem to actively harden Pharaoh's heart until after the sixth plague, after which Pharaoh had already persisted in rebellion. (Remember, even prior to these events Pharaoh was an evil, godless, idolatrous dictator.) In plagues 8-10, God would execute final judgment by hardening Pharaoh's already unrepentant heart for God's ultimate glory.

Bottom line: It's hard to reconcile man's personal responsibility with the God who clearly takes initiative to "harden" Pharaoh's heart. But understanding the ample number of times Pharaoh hardened his own heart first before God ever stepped in shows that yes, we have a choice, but God knows man's true heart condition and will use it for His glory and the good of His people. Exodus is a clear example of how both God's intervening activity and Pharaoh's personal responsibility are indeed present, even if that's difficult to understand.

the little foxes

During my daughter's first grade year, I went on a field trip with her to a local farm. The kids enjoyed the farm animals and even got to feed them. In one particular area, the leader told them they could feed all the animals except the foxes. I watched those foxes, and their ferocity frightened me a bit. I, for one, was thankful for their cage as they hissed and yelped and growled at the children.

Song of Solomon 2:15 says, "Catch the foxes for us, the little foxes that spoil the vineyards, for our vineyards are in blossom." Tucked in the middle of a love story, the bride-to-be wanted to ensure the "little issues" were dealt with swiftly in their blooming romance. She knew that small things can quickly destroy.

> In this passage, God offered Moses four assurances:
>
> 1. His word—that the ones in Egypt who formerly wanted to kill him were dead.
>
> 2. His discipline—a confirmation that He would not allow Moses to walk in disobedience, knowing that disobedience would prevent God's presence from going with him.
>
> 3. His leading—by bringing Aaron to him.
>
> 4. The acceptance of the people—which He had already promised Moses.

What might seem like a "small thing" in Moses' refusal to circumcise his son on the eighth day, as God had commanded, threatened to destroy this blossoming relationship between God and His people. How could God use a man who refused this one act of obedience?

Though we may see God's swift dealings with Moses' sin as overkill, God would not tolerate disobedience, even in an issue that may have seemed small to Moses. What may seem a small issue to us is huge to God. We tend to use ourselves as the standard instead of our Holy Lord. This was true of Moses and his people, and it's true of us.

application

In our journey to freedom, we must understand that we will not walk in freedom while simultaneously walking in disobedience. In fact, the "little foxes" are those that keep us bound in more ways than we recognize.

What "little foxes" in your life might you be passing over or ignoring?

....

....

....

....

....

....

....

....

....

What steps can you make today to deal with them (confess them, change direction) and move forward in freedom?

prayer ~ reflection ~ gratitude

to-do today

Week 2 Day 3
Exodus 5:1-9

Observations ~ Main Points ~ Questions ~ Application:

....
....
....
....
....
....
....

HISTORICAL BACKGROUND

The Pharaoh here was not the same Pharaoh as we saw in chapter 1 (the one who tried to eliminate the Hebrew race). Remember, at least 80 years had passed between chapter 1 and chapter 5. Both Moses and Aaron were in their 80s at this point.

IN CONTEXT

This Pharaoh viewed Israel quite differently than did his genocidal predecessor. He viewed the Hebrew people as a commodity to be used for his personal and his kingdom's gain.

symbols & types

Pharaoh represents a "type" of Satan, or the "god of this world." He demands worship, defiles God, and enslaves God's people.

chained by busyness

What do you do with your free moments? Scroll social media? Seek fleeting pleasure? Entertain yourself?

Pharaoh rationalized that the Hebrew people's dreams of freedom could only result from idleness and excessive free time. So he thought if he could keep them busy, they would have no time, energy, or resources to dream of freedom.

> The busier we are, the less likely we will spend time in worship and in prayer -- leading to disconnection with God and ineffectiveness in our lives.

Pharaoh and Moses both knew something we miss, I'm afraid: Worship and slavery cannot coexist. As long as Pharaoh could keep the Israelites in bondage, busy, and occupied with other concerns, they could not leave his grip and they could not worship.

If we think about it, our enemy doesn't work all that differently. He knows we are most dangerous when we have white space in our lives. It's within our quiet times of prayer and Bible study that God works in us to free us from our areas of bondage and lead us to worship in freedom.

Like Pharaoh, our enemy knows the busier he keeps us, the less likely we will spend time in worship and in prayer. We'll remain disconnected from God and ineffective in our lives.

Sometimes our bondage takes the form of run-of-the-mill busyness. But it probably goes deeper than that for many of us. It's not just busyness but also what we do with those extra free moments.

application

What do you fill your free moments with? Depending on your stage of life, those occasions may look as tiny as the pause at a stoplight or as large as a free weekend. List below how you currently use your free moments:

If I have less than an hour:

....

....

If I have a few hours:

....

....

If I have more time:

....

....

Are there activities or commitments you need to cut back on, to free you to worship in larger blocks of time -- whether on your own, with a group, or in your church?

What about the smaller slices of time? How can you become more intentional to keep those free moments "free" to allow God to speak to your heart?

....

....

FURTHER APPLICATION

Like Pharaoh, your slave driver doesn't care about you or your God. He only cares about the work you do for him and keeping you under his thumb. What "work" might you be doing that is keeping you enslaved and away from worship?

....
....
....

prayer ~ reflection ~ gratitude

to-do today

Week 2 Day 4
Exodus 5:10 - 6:1

Observations ~ Main Points ~ Questions ~ Application:

....
....
....
....
....
....

HISTORICAL BACKGROUND

Straw, when mixed with clay and sand, reinforced the bricks and helped the mixture to stick to the forms. Straw made the work easier and more efficient. Without straw, no doubt, the work proved not only more difficult, but without reinforcement many of the bricks would crumble.

definition
Stubble: It made a poor substitute for straw, rendering the bricks more brittle, therefore making the work more difficult.

when pain obscures hope

My left leg throbbing, I watched my daughter on the soccer field, and I could not even focus on her. With a herniated disc in my back, I couldn't wait until practice ended and I could go home and lie on my stomach, where the pain would ease just a bit.

Hope for a pain-free life seemed to slip away. All I wanted was just a moment of relief.

Israel's foremen found themselves in a similar situation. Just a few verses earlier in 4:31, we can assume they worshipped God and hoped for freedom just like the rest. But when the oppression increased, hope for ultimate freedom faded away. All they wanted to do was ease the pain—even temporarily.

Taking matters into their own hands, the foremen tried to stand up for themselves by appealing to Pharaoh. Their complaints fell on deaf ears, and their pleas echoed back to them empty. As a result, they lashed out at Moses and Aaron, the very ones sent to help secure their freedom.

Likewise, sometimes we can't see past our current circumstances to even imagine what true, lasting freedom would be like. We just want the pain to ease in the moment.

And many times, in the midst of the pain, we blame God or lash out at those God sends to help us.

As a result of the harsh oppression, the Israelites' pain and anger veiled God's promises of freedom.

> Moses questioned God in three ways:
>
> 1. God's *goodness*:
> "Why have you caused trouble for the people?"
>
> 2. God's *purpose*:
> "Why did you send me?"
>
> 3. God's *actions*:
> "You haven't delivered on your promise."
>
> In which of these areas are you most likely to question God?

application

Have you ever felt pain so deeply that you couldn't see past it? When your former hope vanishes, freedom no longer seems within reach.

Like the Israelites, consider the temptations we face when our pain becomes unbearable.

> 1. We take the situation into our own hands. We can't secure freedom -- or even relief from our pain -- on our own. Our only hope is a rescuer, a deliverer.

> 2. We lash out at the people God puts in our lives. When the enemy sees God's deliverance coming near, he amps up his game. Part of his strategy is to separate us from those God sends to help us find freedom.

What is the condition of your freedom? Have you lost hope in finding lasting freedom? Do you find yourself settling for only one more day of survival? If so, what means do you seek to ease (or numb) the pain on your own? Are those effective?

....

....

....

....

....

....

Instead of turning to what is not effective and only leaves you empty, take a step of faith and admit to God that you cannot find freedom on your own. Then trust Him to rescue and deliver you.

Who are your Moses and Aaron right now? Name two people in your life whom you know God has placed in your path to help you in your walk with Him. Share with them this week what God has been teaching you in this study so far.

....

....

....

....

....

FURTHER APPLICATION

As a result of Pharaoh's command, Exodus 5:12 says the people "scattered throughout the land of Egypt to gather stubble for straw." At the time, the Israelites lived in their own land of Goshen, separated from the paganistic Egyptians. Due to this edict, they were forced to "scatter" throughout Egypt. As a result, they left the protection of their people -- even for just a part of the day, and integrated with the people of Egypt.

From a New Testament perspective, Egypt represents the world. When we find ourselves under oppression (from without or within), we may find ourselves "scattering" from God's protection -- gathering sustenance from the world instead of from the haven of God's people. Just like stubble proved a poor substitute for straw, what the world gives us will always prove a poor substitute for what we gain from the fellowship with other believers.

When we are oppressed or in bondage of any sort, we face the temptation to scatter from God's people. This could take the form of withdrawing from our local church. Or it might mean attending church but not letting ourselves become invested in person-to-person relationships and accountability. We withdraw from fellowship into anonymity and isolation.

When we scatter from our local church, we feed from the world's table. We're satisfied with stubble instead of straw, yet wonder why our proverbial bricks keep crumbling.

God's people aren't perfect. We'll definitely see this in the coming weeks as we look at Israel. But we are God's people, and He uses His people to help His people. He uses His people as the means to comfort and rescue us in our times of need. Resist the temptation to scatter, to disengage from your local fellowship of believers. They need us, and we need them.

The opposite of "to scatter" is "to gather." Do you need to make a fresh commitment to "gather" together with your local church?

prayer ~ reflection ~ gratitude

to-do today

Week 2 Day 5
Exodus 6:2-27

Observations ~ Main Points ~ Questions ~ Application:

HISTORICAL BACKGROUND

The term "outstretched arm" usually described Pharaoh in the Egyptian context. By using this description of Himself, God set the stage for His victory over Pharaoh.

IN CONTEXT

What did God mean when He said in verse 3, "I was not known to them by my name 'the LORD '"? God's name, translated "Yahweh, or LORD," had in fact been revealed to both Abraham (Genesis 15:7-21) and Jacob (Genesis 28:13-15).

But, in both of these examples, God was revealing and confirming to Abraham and Jacob His covenant to bring their offspring back to Canaan.

In Exodus 6:3, God essentially said, "What they were told, you're about to see." The name Yahweh (the LORD) revealed God as a promise keeper.

IN CONTEXT

Moses' objection in verse 12 did not use the same language as the objection we saw in 3:10. Instead, the literal translation here is "uncircumcised lips." Perhaps this objection connotes an understanding of Moses' own heart condition as morally unclean. Perhaps, in light of God's revelation of His name and what it meant, he felt incapable of fulfilling such a grand task. Again, God took the focus off Moses' insecurities and placed it back on what He was about to do.

DIG DEEPER

The purpose of the genealogy in verses 14-27 was to identify Moses and Aaron as descendants of Levi. "Sons" in verse 18 can mean descendants. Amram in verse 18 is probably not the Amram in verse 20 (more than 2 generations would have passed in the 400 years in Egypt between Levi and Moses).

failure despite obedience

Night after night I left my son's room deflated. Another conversation about salvation. Another night when he struggled to make the heart connection. Why is this so hard?

I tried to do everything "right" with my son, my firstborn -- even things that seem a bit over the top now. (I read the Bible to my pregnant tummy, for one.) But as days turned to years and head knowledge of salvation couldn't seem to find its way to his heart, I left his room many nights in despair.

Then it occurred to me. What if everything in his walk with the Lord occurred on my timetable, just as I would have wanted it? Would I have taken credit?

As the years went on, I realized I could do nothing. It would all have to be God.

That was the point! It's all about Him!

Moses did everything God commanded him to do, yet his first attempt failed. Why would God do that to him? Scripture doesn't tell us, but I have to wonder if the purpose was for God to show a helpless Moses and a hopeless Israel that deliverance would only come from one Source -- God Himself.

In today's text we see that Moses wasn't the only one frustrated with this blow. The people of Israel, who had first believed Moses and God, did not believe God now. Even after multiple promises from God (v. 6-8), their broken spirits blocked their belief.

symbols & types

Consider these New Testament correlations to four concepts:

1. Any time the "forced labor of the Egyptians" is mentioned, this corresponds to our slavery to sin.

2. "Redeem" means to buy back. Jesus redeemed us by offering Himself as payment for our debt, allowing us to come to a relationship with God.

3. Many scholars believe "the land" (the Promised Land) corresponds to our lives with Jesus in a place of freedom. This life begins when a person receives Christ but extends into eternity.

4. Israel represents Christians. We are delivered from the bondage of the world, and led on a pilgrim journey by God Himself.

application

Sometimes God doesn't appear to keep His promises -- not in the way and timing we expect, anyway. How do we respond? Do we stop believing? Do we give up hope? Do we turn away from Him and from His word?

When has God not come through in the manner you expected, and you've found yourself tempted to give up and stop believing His promises? List them below.

....

....

....

....

Sometimes the chains that hold us captive take the form of resentment toward God. Though we don't always know the "why" behind His ways, He gives us His promises to sustain us.

Write each of the "I will" promises in verses 6-8 below:

....

....

....

....

....

....

Which speak most deeply to your heart?

....

....

....

Ask God to help you understand and believe these promises—even when His ways don't always seem clear. Even when they don't line up with your own expectations.

FURTHER APPLICATION

Perhaps Moses blamed himself for the lack of success at the first attempt with Pharaoh. When things don't go the way we hope -- even if it's something we feel God has asked us to do -- do we blame ourselves? Just like with Moses and the Israelites, things can get worse before they get better. But there's always a purpose in the life of a believer. Ultimately, that purpose is so that God's glory can be displayed and so that we will know He is God. How does this give us hope when we're tempted to blame ourselves for failure?

....

....

....

....

....

prayer ~ reflection ~ gratitude

to-do today

Week 3 Day 1
Exodus 6:28 - 7:13

Observations ~ Main Points ~ Questions ~ Application:

....

....

....

....

....

....

HISTORICAL BACKGROUND

The Ten Plagues (which we will begin exploring tomorrow), likely took place within a span of about nine months. We know this based on the agricultural and weather patterns of the area:

- The first plague took place when the Nile rises, which is in July and August.

- The seventh plague occurred when the barley ripened and the flax blossomed, which is in January.

- The eighth plague coincided with the yearly east winds in March and April.

- The tenth judgment -- the Passover -- took place in April.

definition

A sign validates a claim that a person had been sent by God for those who already believed in God. A wonder authenticates the sender and his message to those who do not believe in God. Thus, signs were given to show Israel that Moses was a messenger of God, and wonders were given to Pharaoh and the Egyptians to show them that God was the true God.

HISTORICAL BACKGROUND

As we look at each of the Ten Plagues, understand that each judgment smashed some aspect of Egypt's religious life and specifically the gods they followed. We will look more into that with each plague.

CROSS-REFERENCE

Most likely the miracles the magicians performed (v. 11-12) were empowered by Satan. Second Thessalonians 2:9 says, "The coming of the lawless one is based on Satan's working, with all kinds of false miracles, signs, and wonders..."

According to 2 Timothy 3:8, the magicians' names were Jannes and Jambres: "Just as Jannes and Jambres resisted Moses, so these also resist the truth. They are men who are corrupt in mind and worthless in regard to the faith."

the wrong question

"You're asking the wrong question."

Has anyone ever said that to you? It's happened to me, and it's not enjoyable. I had to take a red-faced step back and admit I just wasn't "getting it."

At the beginning of today's text we see Moses' familiar objection, "Since I am such a poor speaker, how will Pharaoh listen to me?" (6:29) Thus far, we've looked at Moses' objection and his excuse of poor speaking ability, but today, let's look at the question, "How will Pharaoh listen to me?"

Moses was asking the wrong question. And we see this by God's reply in Exodus 7:4: "Pharaoh will not listen to you" (emphasis mine).

All along in God's dialogue with him, Moses had missed the point. In his view, the key to Israel's release resided in Pharaoh's hands. How could freedom come without Pharaoh's consent? But God had no intention of Pharaoh lifting a finger to help the Israelites. No, God had bigger plans, much greater than Moses could imagine.

Could it be that we, like Moses, ask the wrong questions at times? We see a pharaoh blocking our road to freedom and think if our pharaoh would step aside, we could get to our destination.

We think:
If this person would accept me...
If finances were more secure...
If someone would just notice me...
If my husband supported me...
If that person would just ask for forgiveness...
If I lost my craving for substance or overindulgence...

...then we could know freedom.

When we view life through this myopic lens, as Moses did, we see our huge pharaoh standing in the way. We can't fathom God rescuing us by any other means.

But God doesn't want to be the key that unlocks our pharaoh. He wants to demolish the roadblock! He wants to lead us into freedom in such a cataclysmic fashion that we will know that our Lord IS God! Our personal pharaohs don't compare to His power and might.

application

What are the pharaohs in your life? In other words, what outside influences block you from moving from where you are to where you want to be? Possibly, from where God wants you to be?

....

....

Read Exodus 6:30 and 7:4 side by side. How might God's response to Moses change your prayers concerning these influences?

....

....

prayer ~ reflection ~ gratitude

....
....
....
....
....
....

to-do today

....
....

Week 3 Day 2
Exodus 7:14-25

Observations ~ Main Points ~ Questions ~ Application:

....

....

....

....

....

....

....

HISTORICAL BACKGROUND

The Nile River, the source of Egypt's livelihood, represented life and was regarded as a god to the Egyptians. Annually, when it overflowed its banks, it brought fertile silt, which made crops and livestock flourish. "The silt's fertilizing power has been calculated at $85.36 an acre. (By way of comparison, it costs an average of $5.43 today to fertilize an acre of soybeans.)" (Feiler, Walking through the Bible)

IN CONTEXT

Hapi and Isis, the Egyptian god and goddess of the Nile, could not prevent or reverse this tragedy. In this first plague, the Egyptians began to see the impotency of their gods and the power of the one true God.

CROSS-REFERENCE

Flip to the following passages in Exodus: 5:2, 6:7, 7:5, and 16:12. Repeatedly, God says, "You will know that I am Yahweh." This contrasts with the gods of the Egyptians and answers the question of why it was necessary to bring these ten plagues in this way.

On that day I swore to them that I would bring them out of the land of Egypt into a land I had searched out for them, a land flowing with milk and honey, the most beautiful of all lands. I also said to them, "Throw away, each of you, the abhorrent things that you prize, and do not defile yourselves with the idols of Egypt. I am the Lord your God."

But they rebelled against me and were unwilling to listen to me. None of them threw away the abhorrent things that they prized, and they did not abandon the idols of Egypt. So I considered pouring out my wrath on them, exhausting my anger against them within the land of Egypt. But I acted for the sake of my name, so that it would not be profaned in the eyes of the nations they were living among, in whose sight I had made myself known to Israel by bringing them out of Egypt. (Ezekiel 20:6-9)

CROSS-REFERENCE

Although Israel was primarily segregated, they had begun to assimilate the idols of Egypt to themselves. According to Ezekiel 20:6-9 (in the margin), God recounted having told the Israelites to throw away the idols of Egypt. He wanted no contamination among His people.

CROSS-REFERENCE

The magicians sought to imitate God's work by producing counterfeit miracles. Satan uses the same tactics in the New Testament and today. Look up some of the examples of Satan's counterfeits:
- 2 Corinthians 11:26 (False Christians)
- Galatians 1:6-9 (Imitation gospel)
- Romans 10:1-3 (Counterfeit righteousness)
- 2 Corinthians 11:13-15 (Counterfeit ministers)

DIG DEEPER

The purposes of the ten plagues were three-fold:

1. Signs to Israel: The Israelites had heard of God but they had not heard from Him in generations. By demonstrating His power through the plagues, God showed Israel who He was and demonstrated His power and care over them.

2. Judgments to Egypt: Not only were the Egyptians judged for their worship of false gods, but God used the plagues to punish their mistreatment of His people.

3. Prophecies of Judgments to Come: In the book of Revelation, judgments of future plagues bear a remarkable resemblance to the plagues in Egypt. (Revelation 8:8, 16:2-6, 16:13, 8:7, 9:1, 16:10)

the powerlessness of counterfeit righteousness

Today's generation of young adults has sloughed off legalism like an old pair of shoes, but I believe they still want to know when they've done things "right." That human trait just looks different from generation to generation.

For example, Baby Boomers value faithful church attendance and respect for authority, while Millennials esteem social responsibility and justice. All are good, necessary, and even biblical. At the core, though, these virtues only prove as good as the heart motives behind them.

When our hearts aren't right, even good things serve as counterfeits for real fruit that comes from Jesus Himself and the Spirit's work in our lives. We can't manufacture that on our own any more than the magicians could consistently copy the plagues of God.

In Romans 10:3, Paul spoke of Israel as a nation, but I think we can identify as well. "Since they are ignorant of the righteousness of God and attempted to establish their own righteousness, they have not submitted to God's righteousness."

Like the magicians in Egypt, we can counterfeit God's good things and seek to establish our own righteousness, sometimes without realizing it.

And until we recognize the powerlessness of this counterfeit righteousness, we'll remain enslaved to it.

application

Let's examine some ways we might attempt to establish our own counterfeit version of righteousness without being aware of it. Here are a few examples from the fruit of the Spirit (Gal. 5:22-23). Check the statement that describes you most accurately in daily life. (You may check one, both, or neither for each line.)

To my family:

LOVE: ____ I show love
____ I genuinely do love

JOY: ____ My demeanor is joyful
____ I feel joy in my heart

PEACE: ____ I act at peace
____ I am at peace

PATIENCE: ____ I exercise patience outwardly
____ I am patient inwardly

KINDNESS: ____ I am nice
____ I am kind

To others:

LOVE: ____ I show love
____ I genuinely do love

JOY: ____ My demeanor is joyful
____ I feel joy in my heart

PEACE: ____ I act at peace
              ____ I am at peace

PATIENCE: ____ I exercise patience outwardly
              ____ I am patient inwardly

KINDNESS: ____ I am nice
              ____ I am kind

Review each question. Do you believe your heart and actions line up? If they don't, this may be something you need to take to God. Perhaps this is an area where you find yourself in bondage. Or depending on how you answer these questions, it may show a need to examine your heart. Could you be guilty of manufacturing your own version of righteousness? Perhaps it indicates that your heart may not be right with God in this area.

This exercise, of course, is only a starting point. My intent is to assist in determining areas of counterfeit righteousness in your own life. Like I said, many of us have such areas without even realizing it.

With that in mind, has God shown you areas where you have attempted to establish your own righteousness? In other words, in what areas might you be trying to be "good enough" on your own merit?

> My reason for separating this activity into two areas -- family and others -- is due to our tendency to feel and behave differently with our family than with those who are not part of our immediate family.

....

....

....

prayer ~ reflection ~ gratitude

to-do today

Week 3 Day 3
Exodus 8:1-27

Observations ~ Main Points ~ Questions ~ Application:

....

....

....

....

....

....

....

HISTORICAL BACKGROUND

As a polytheistic nation, the Egyptians worshipped many gods who represented different forces of nature. For example, Heqet was the Egyptian goddess of fertility who also symbolized resurrection. The Egyptians likened her to a woman with a frog's head. But as their gods repeatedly failed to protect them from the plagues, the Egyptian people began to see the powerlessness of their gods in contrast with the Hebrew God's power and might. Not merely a foreign nation's god, God proved Himself as the creator and sustainer of all the earth, not to be counted among many gods but to be viewed as the one and only true God.

IN CONTEXT

When Moses told Pharaoh in the second plague to "pick a time" for the frogs to stop, he showed that God could start and stop a plague at will. This demonstrated the supernatural nature of the plagues and crushed any accusations that their causes were merely from natural forces.

HISTORICAL BACKGROUND

The Hebrew word translated as "fly" is a bit obscure and difficult to translate. Contemporary Christian scholars have translated it as a fly, beetle, or even more likely, a mosquito. The literal word seems to mean "swarm." Hebrew interpreters generally believe it meant wild beasts or "noxious beasts" such as scorpions or even snakes. The fact that Pharaoh was so desperate for a reprieve, finally starting to offer compromises with Moses, may indicate that this plague was much more troublesome than the flies we might think of.

IN CONTEXT

The third plague was the first one the Egyptian magicians could not replicate, but even when they stated the plague only came by the "finger of God," they did not use the Hebrew word for God. That would have acknowledged the deity of the God of Israel and denied the deity of Pharaoh. But as even Pharaoh recognized the gods of nature, the magicians pointed to "a" god who brought this plague, not "the" God.

DIG DEEPER

In the initiation of the fourth plague, God shielded Israel from the plagues for the first time. In verse 23, the word "distinction" literally means redemption, ransom, or deliverance. This lays the foundation for understanding that the covering from judgment (salvation) is something won on our behalf, not something we earn.

sacrificing the valuables

As a fan of Christian fiction, I'm amazed at the popularity of Amish Christian fiction, about people living separate from the world. What is it about this simple lifestyle that appeals to us?

The reality is, most of us live in the midst of the world, shoulder to shoulder. And if we take Jesus' command in the Great Commission seriously, we actively engage that world with the gospel of Christ.

But unfortunately -- and more likely -- the world rubs off on us more than we rub off on the world. That's why we may see Pharaoh's first compromise as not such a bad idea. In verse 25, Pharaoh agreed to let the Israelites sacrifice to God (worship) but only if they stayed in Egypt.

> We can't worship God while our hearts belong to the world.

What's wrong with worship in Egypt?

The answer lies in verses 26-27. Our God and the gods of the world clash.

As New Testament believers, this concept speaks more to our hearts than to our physical location. We can't worship God while our hearts belong to the world.

Just as the Egyptians worshipped and valued the animals the Israelites would sacrifice, so also the things we're called to sacrifice are the very things beloved by the world around us.

application

Look at some of the things we're called to sacrifice as believers in Christ -- things that are valuable to the world:

• Self: "[Jesus] instead...emptied himself by assuming the form of a servant..." Philippians 2:7a

• Money/possessions: "No one can serve two masters, since either he will hate one and love the other, or he will be devoted to one and despise the other. You cannot serve both God and money." Matthew 6:24

• Reputation: "Do nothing out of selfish ambition or conceit, but in humility consider others as more important than yourselves." Philippians 2:3

• Life: "For whoever wants to save his life will lose it, but whoever loses his life because of me will find it." Matthew 16:25

• Body: "Therefore, brothers and sisters, in view of the mercies of God, I urge you to present your bodies as a living sacrifice, holy and pleasing to God; this is your true worship." Romans 12:1

• Pride in personal success: "But everything that was a gain to me, I have considered to be a loss because of Christ." Philippians 3:7

Are you trying to worship God while remaining in "Egypt" in any of these areas? Are you holding on to idols belonging to "Egypt"? How might God be calling you "out" so you can worship and serve Him wholeheartedly?

....

....

FURTHER APPLICATION

When Scripture describes Pharaoh in verse 14 as having hardened his heart, the Hebrew word/phrase here is different than is used in other instances. It indicates a continuous willful stubbornness as he conditioned his own heart, a requirement for him to refuse to recant in the face this particular plague.

Take note of times when you might willfully condition your heart to harden in a particular situation, especially when you see God calling for repentance. The result of a willfully conditioned stubborn heart is a hard heart that only gets harder. When our hearts reach this point, not only are we out of step with the will of God, but resentment and rebellion take root, and bondage then creeps into many other areas of our lives.

prayer ~ reflection ~ gratitude

to-do today

Week 3 Day 4

Exodus 8:28 - 9:35

Observations ~ Main Points ~ Questions ~ Application:

HISTORICAL BACKGROUND

Many of the animals killed in the fifth plague were considered sacred in Egyptian polytheism -- Apis was the god of the bull; Hathor was the god of the cow; and Khnum was the god of the ram. In addition, the Egyptians worshipped three gods with "power" over disease, yet they could not stop the painful boils. This was yet another example of the Egyptian people observing the powerlessness of their gods.

Because the Egyptians worshipped animals, the flocks were said to have been kept outside of the main cities -- mainly in Goshen where the Israelites lived -- and thus their flocks mingled with the Israelites' flocks. This made the survival of the Jewish animals all that more profound since they shared the same resources (air, water, pasture) with the animals belonging to the Egyptians.

CROSS-REFERENCE

When Pharaoh admitted that he had "sinned," this is the same word he used in Exodus 5:16, when he accused the Israelites of being "at fault" by not making enough bricks. His subsequent actions indicate an unchanged, unrepentant heart, which contributed to further sin (v. 34).

DIG DEEPER

What Egyptian animals are referred to in 9:9 and 9:19 if all of the animals had been killed in the fifth plague (9:6)? Several explanations have been proposed:

1. Only the animals mentioned in 9:3 were killed
2. Only the animals "in the field" (9:3) suffered from the plague but the ones under shelter remained
3. The Egyptians acquired more animals either from Israel or from other sources
4. The swath statement "all" is meant as hyperbole, indicating the scope of the plague not the exact number of deaths.

DIG DEEPER

The plagues can be divided into three sets of three. In each set, God warned Pharaoh of the first two plagues but the third did not come with a warning. This hints that the first two may have given Pharaoh (and the Egyptians) opportunity to repent, while the third was simply punishment.

not too far

Seated in the balcony, my family and I observed countless church members make their way to the front, laying hands on a young woman preparing to journey as a missionary to an area hostile to Christianity.

My seven-year-old daughter sat beside me and I thought, "What if that were my daughter?" Would I, after teaching her to follow God all her life, encourage her to go all out for Jesus?

Yesterday we saw Pharaoh's first offered compromise to Moses: "Sacrifice to God within the country." Today, we see his second offered compromise: I will let you go, but don't go very far.

How often might the enemy tempt us with the same compromise? Go, but don't go very far.

This very real and dangerous compromise snakes into the fibers of our own hearts and lifestyle before we even realize it.

Follow God, but not too far. Don't go getting crazy or fanatical. Think logically.

For most of us, we're not wrestling with a call of God to journey to a far-off land (though don't discount it). But the temptation is just the same. We want to follow God, but not too far.

We'll follow, as long as it's comfortable. As long as we don't have to do anything hard. As long as we're not asked to sacrifice too much.

Just as the Israelites would never have found their way to lasting freedom by "not going too far," we won't either. We find the freedom Christ offers when we follow wherever He leads.

application

In what areas are you tempted to say, "Not too far, Lord"? Be honest with yourself. Be honest with God.

....

....

....

....

In the margin, list your fears and struggles in these areas. Ask Him to help you let go and follow Him, near or far.

prayer ~ reflection ~ gratitude

to-do today

Week 3 Day 5
Exodus 10

Observations ~ Main Points ~ Questions ~ Application:

HISTORICAL BACKGROUND

Egyptians worshipped Nut, the sky goddess and Osiris, the god of crop fertility, neither of which could spare them from the plague of locusts. The plague of darkness had particular implications on Pharaoh, as he was thought to be a son of Re, the sun god. Yet he could not control the darkness either.

IN CONTEXT

What looked like mercy in the seventh plague -- the wheat and spelt crops spared -- became judgment in their destruction during the eighth plague of locusts.

CROSS-REFERENCE

In Exodus 9:25 we are told the hail "shattered every tree in the field." So what was there left for the locusts to eat in 10:5? Most likely the trees began to regrow and leaf out, but this regrowth was soon decimated by the locusts.

DIG DEEPER

Multiple times Pharaoh confessed but at no time did he change his posture toward Israel or his actions. Thus we see a glaring example. Confession that doesn't lead to repentance is insincere. The true test of a repentant heart is found in the attitudes and actions that follow.

DIG DEEPER

In addition to keeping Israel together during their journey out of Egypt, other reasons it was unacceptable to leave the women and children in Egypt while the elders and men worshipped the Lord in the wilderness can be postulated: (1) In God's ideal plan, whole families will follow the Lord together, (2) leaving women and children in Egypt would have left them vulnerable to violence and crime at the hands of the Egyptians without the Israelite men to protect them, and (3) men are not the only ones accountable and expected to worship and sacrifice to the Lord; women bear an equally binding responsibility in their personal relationships with God.

holding back

My dad drove up to my apartment in a U-Haul truck. As we unrolled the door, I saw my childhood bedroom furniture inside. I remembered when as a young child this same set arrived brand new. Now I was a sophomore in college moving into my own apartment two hours away from home.

Though I had lived in a residence hall and a furnished on-campus apartment for a year and a half, the arrival of my furniture represented permanence -- both for my parents and for me.

I would never live in my parents' home again.

Pharaoh seemed to begin wearing down with the devastating plagues, and thus far, his first two compromises were met with refusal. Then, with the eighth and ninth plague he offered two more. In the first attempt, only the men could go worship the Lord, and in the second, the people could go but not the flocks and herds.

Neither compromise was acceptable, of course, because God had called Israel to a permanent freedom, not a temporary respite. Pharaoh knew if he could convince the Israelites to leave their families or possessions, he could ensure their return.

When Jesus beckons us to follow Him to freedom, He calls us to give the whole of our lives. But sometimes we attempt to make the same compromises Pharaoh proposed. We'll give God part of ourselves but leave some parts out.

The potential to leave a part of ourselves in Egypt and not take our whole selves with Jesus into freedom exists in countless areas of our lives.

In Matthew 6:21 Jesus says, "For where your treasure is, there your heart will be also." God knows we can't serve two masters.

application

Are you leaving part of yourself, your heart, or your treasure in Egypt? Ask God to show you the areas, people or obedience you're withholding from Him. List these areas below.

....

....

....

prayer ~ reflection ~ gratitude

to-do today

Week 4 Day 1
Exodus 11

Observations ~ Main Points ~ Questions ~ Application:

....

....

....

....

....

....

HISTORICAL BACKGROUND

With this final plague, the Egyptians' goddess Isis, the supposed protector of children, could not protect the firstborn of the Egyptians from this terror.

CROSS-REFERENCE

The word "make a distinction" is only used seven times in the Old Testament -- four of those times in Exodus. The other three are found in Psalms. Look up these verses in Psalms and consider their meaning in light of this word's use in Exodus:

- Psalm 4:3 (the word translated "set apart")
- Psalm 17:7 (the phrase translated "display wonder")
- Psalm 139:14 (the word translated "wonderfully made")

CROSS-REFERENCE

When God told the Israelites to ask the Egyptians for gold and silver, He fulfilled the promise made to Abraham concerning this very event in Genesis 15:14: "I will judge the nation they serve, and afterward they will go out with many possessions."

CROSS-REFERENCE

If this tenth plague seems unusually harsh, read Romans 1:18-23 in the margin. Unbelief brings judgment upon itself. Even after all the wonders revealed to them, the Egyptians refused to worship the true God.

DIG DEEPER

Why was the final plague the death of the firstborns? Could this allude to God's rejection of our first birth, since we are born into sin? Jesus told Nicodemus he must be "born again" (John 3:3), rendering our first birth inadequate. Interestingly, the rejection of the "firstborn" can be seen in other notable families:

- God rejected Cain, Adam's firstborn, and accepted Abel and subsequently Seth

- God rejected Ishmael, Abraham's firstborn, and accepted Isaac

- God rejected Esau, Isaac's firstborn, and accepted Jacob, from whose line the nation of Israel came

- God rejected Saul, Israel's first earthly king, and subsequently installed David as a forerunner to Jesus

- Paul also speaks of God's rejection of the first Adam (Adam) and acceptance of the second Adam, (Christ). (See 1 Corinthians 15:45-49.)

For God's wrath is revealed from heaven against all godlessness and unrighteousness of people who by their unrighteousness suppress the truth, since what can be known about God is evident among them, because God has shown it to them. For his invisible attributes, that is, his eternal power and divine nature, have been clearly seen since the creation of the world, being understood through what he has made. As a result, people are without excuse. For though they knew God, they did not glorify him as God or show gratitude. Instead, their thinking became worthless, and their senseless hearts were darkened. Claiming to be wise, they became fools and exchanged the glory of the immortal God for images resembling mortal man, birds, four-footed animals, and reptiles. (Romans 1:18-23)

a distinction

What distinguishes us from other people? We might think of our country of origin, education, vocation, appearance, convictions, political ideologies, you name it. But have you ever considered that God distinguishes between you (as His child) and others?

To this point, we've seen hints of how God, in His execution of the plagues, differentiated between Israel and Egypt.

As we move on to chapter 11, when God warned Moses of the final plague, we see this phrase again in 11:7. This Hebrew word translated as "make a distinction" is only used a handful of times in Scripture, but its use tells us it's a pretty powerful concept -- a concept we can directly connect to our walk with Christ today.

> ## definition
> The Hebrew word translated as "make a distinction" can also mean set apart, make wonderful, or mark out.

First, Israel did nothing to earn this distinction, just like we do nothing to earn God's favor upon us. In Exodus 33:16, when this phrase is used again, it's God's presence alone that "makes the distinction" between Israel and the other nations. Similarly, the Holy Spirit's work in us will distinguish and set us apart as God's people.

Second, not only did this distinction become part of their identity as God's people, but it implied a responsibility on their part. As a people set apart by God and for Him, there was no question about whether they would obey God's leading. They followed because they were His and they saw the way He spared them from judgment.

When we trust Christ as our Savior and deliverer, we immediately identify as His and our response should be the same: obedience.

application

Have you considered that God makes a distinction between you and those who aren't His? Spend some time thanking God for delivering you and praise Him for making you His child.

FURTHER APPLICATION

The word "make a distinction" was also used in the fifth plague -- the death of livestock -- where the Israelite livestock were said to have been set apart. Likewise, in foretelling the tenth plague -- the death of the firstborn -- the firstborn of the Egyptian animals would die as well.

Why would animals be subject to judgment, and why would the animals be distinguished in a similar way as the people were?

These animals were gods to the Egyptians; thus, both the people and their false gods received judgment.

What does this tell us about good things in our lives that may become gods to us?

....

....

....

....

What good things are present in your life that are, or have the potential to become, a god in your life?

....

....

....

....

prayer ~ reflection ~ gratitude

to-do today

Week 4 Day 2
Exodus 12:1-28

Observations ~ Main Points ~ Questions ~ Application:

DIG DEEPER

At the end of Exodus 12:22, Moses gave the command that no one could leave their homes until morning, and leftover meat had to be burned. This prevented Israel from sharing any extra with others who were not part of the community. This points to the truth that Jesus' blood only covers those under its protection. While we can "share" the message of God with another, it's their decision to place themselves under Jesus' saving grace and protection. Jesus is the only shield for the wrath of God for our sin. (John 14:6)

CHRIST IN EXODUS

In today's text we begin to see multiple examples of how the Passover directly points to Christ and His sacrifice for us:

Verse in Exodus	Description	New Testament Correlation	New Testament Passage or Old Testament Prophecy
12:5	Unblemished animal	Christ was perfect, without defect	1 Cor. 5:7, 1 Peter 1:9, 2 Cor. 5:21, 1 Peter 2:22, 1 John 3:5
12:10	Could not save any leftovers because it would ruin	Christ's body did not see corruption (it did not decay)	Psalm 16:10
12:13	The blood of the animal on the doorposts was required to escape death	Christ's blood covers us, allowing us to escape spiritual death	Romans 5:9, Ephesians 1:7
12:9	Roasting over fire	Fire represents judgment or wrath; Jesus endured God's wrath for us.	Galatians 3:13
12:3	Lamb was chosen before it was slain	Jesus was also chosen before He was slain.	1 Peter 1:20
12:6	Lamb had to be tested to ensure it was unblemished	Jesus was tested before His earthly ministry	Matthew 4:1-11
12:46	Lamb's bones could not be broken	Jesus' bones were not broken, despite the custom of crucifixion	John 19:33,36

CHRIST IN EXODUS

Besides direct correlations between the Passover Lamb and Jesus, we see other correlations in the text that point to the new covenant of Jesus Christ:

- A new calendar represented a new national identity for Israel, just as the crucifixion of Jesus represented a new covenant and our new life in Christ, plus the fact that our calendar uses BC and AD. So, His death forever changes the way we measure our time.
- Bitter herbs typified sorrow or grief. For Israel, this would be a reminder of their oppression in Egypt. For us, this is a reminder of our past sin.
- Yeast corresponded with sin; there could be no yeast in the home when the animal was slain, just as followers of Christ are called to rid our lives of sin. Consider Paul's admonishment: "Clean out the old leaven so that you may be a new unleavened batch, as indeed you are. For Christ our Passover lamb has been sacrificed. Therefore, let us observe the feast, not with old leaven or with the leaven of malice and evil, but with the unleavened bread of sincerity and truth," 1 Cor. 5:7-8.
- Hyssop was associated with purification. By Jesus' blood, we are cleansed of our sin.
- Both the Passover animal and Jesus were slain on the fourteenth day of the month.
- Jesus was described in the New Testament as the Lamb of God, (John 1:29, Rev. 5:12).

new beginnings

In August 1998 I moved out of my home and went to college. In August 2001 I married. In June 2002 I started my career. August 2006 was the month I became a mom, and in January 2013 I quit my job to become a stay-at-home mom. Why can I rattle off those dates without a second thought?

Because they each represent new beginnings in my life. With each new beginning, I turned away from living at home, being single, being a student, living without children, and having a vocational career. With major life changes and new beginnings, we recognize life will be different.

Before the tenth plague struck, the Israelites did not realize a new beginning hovered on the horizon, but God did. To prepare them, He instituted a calendar change. Then He began instructing them on specifics regarding this odd meal in which they would take part.

> When we accept the sacrifice of Jesus, our very identity changes!

To this point, the Israelites only observed God's ways from a distance. They believed Moses heard from God. But now, God's ways became personal.

Their way of life -- their very identity -- was about to change!

Why does any of this matter to us? We don't celebrate the Passover each year. We don't rid our homes of yeast and roast a lamb over a fire. How can this mean anything to us today?

Because it means everything. As I hope you're beginning to see, everything about the Israelites' journey to freedom points to our own.

When we accept the sacrifice of Jesus -- the perfect lamb -- for our sins, and we follow Him, it's the new beginning of new beginnings!

Our way of life -- our very identity -- changes!

Even at the time God gave these instructions (which sound strange to our ears), He was thinking of us. Understanding this changes our perspective as we read them.

I remember in my decade working at a Ford dealership, we would read about new models of vehicles coming within the year. We saw pictures of prototypes, diagrams of the interior, and lists of features. But those pictures only took us so far. It wasn't until the vehicle was finally delivered to the dealership that we really understood the pictures we had seen. We could finally drive and experience all we read about.

In a way, that's what Exodus is. It's a picture, a diagram, a list of features representing what would come. The "real thing" came when Jesus fulfilled the prototypes peppered throughout the Old Testament.

The details we read here absolutely apply to our lives. Our salvation. Our own new beginning.

application

As you read Exodus 12:2, think about your own "new beginning." Praise God for what He started in you, then look for pictures of your own faith and walk with God as you continue reading Exodus.

....

....

....

....

prayer ~ reflection ~ gratitude

to-do today

Week 4 Day 3
Exodus 12:29-42

Observations ~ Main Points ~ Questions ~ Application:

HISTORICAL BACKGROUND

Some calculate that 600,000 able-bodied men, plus their wives and children, added to approximately two million Israelites. Two million of God's people left Egypt in their exodus to the wilderness—and freedom.

CROSS-REFERENCE

The mixed crowd caused the Israelites trouble by leading in the complaints. Numbers 11:4 says, "The riffraff among them had a strong craving for other food. The Israelites wept again and said, 'Who will feed us meat?'"

definition

The "mixed crowd" in Exodus 12:38 may have represented Egyptians or foreigners who saw the exodus as a way to escape Egypt.

a new identity: own it

I'll never forget the day I put on the shirt and wore it in public. A stretchy light blue t-shirt, it displayed the name of my church and the words "women's ministry."

The shirt had hung in my closet since the day it was given to me at a women's event weeks ago. I had served in the women's ministry for a few months, but because I was a new member to the church, I struggled to see myself as one of them. What if someone who had been part of the church for years saw me and didn't know me? Did I really fit in? I felt like an imposter.

Then the day came when I finally wore the shirt. I decided to "own it." In a way, it felt like finally accepting a new identity that had already been mine for a long time.

Before the exodus, the people of Israel hadn't known anything but slavery and oppression.

But Exodus 12:37 describes the six hundred thousand men that went out as "able-bodied men on foot." In every other place in the Old Testament where this Hebrew word "man on foot" is found, it's used in the context of battle. In other words, though these men had never known war, God called them soldiers.

Think about it. In the course of a few hours these

> **definition**
>
> The Hebrew word for Passover is pesah, which means a shielding or delivering. The Lord didn't simply "pass over" the Israelite households where He saw the blood. He protected them at the entrance from wrath and judgment.

people found their identities transformed -- from slaves to soldiers!

Of course, God didn't have war planned for them yet (it would come later), but their identity as a people changed. No longer slaves to a foreign, idolatrous entity, now they were soldiers for the Lord God!

As we read in Exodus, Numbers, and Deuteronomy, it took many years and countless foibles for the Israelites to "own" their new identity. But God marked them from the very night He won their freedom.

Sometimes we have trouble "owning" our new identity in Christ. Like me and my t-shirt, we know we have it but we let it sit in our closet. We overlook it in favor of something we know better, something that feels more comfortable. Or we may not put it on because someone might see our imperfections and think we're not what we say we are.

If you are in Christ, Scripture says the old has gone and the new has come (2 Cor. 5:17). The Israelites did nothing to earn their new identity, and neither did you. When you accept it, it's already yours.

application

Is there a part of your identity in Christ that you struggle to "own?" What slave clothes do you go back to again and again?

....

....

....

FURTHER APPLICATION

Among God's people we will always find a "mixed crowd" -- those who identify with God's people but inwardly aren't children of God. These are ones who lead in complaint and try to lead God's people astray. Though we cannot always do anything about this negative influence (see Jesus' words about the wheat and the tares in Matthew 13:24-40), we can control whether they influence us. Keep watch for this "mixed crowd." Like the "riffraff" in Numbers 11:4, they prompt you to grumble and complain, promote an ungrateful spirit, and above all, remove your focus from the God who set you free.

prayer ~ reflection ~ gratitude

to-do today

Week 4 Day 4
Exodus 12:43-51

Observations ~ Main Points ~ Questions ~ Application:

HISTORICAL BACKGROUND

The word translated "foreigner" in 12:43 is actually two separate Hebrew words. One of those words means "son" and the other means "foreigner" or "alien." According to the Chumash, a Jewish commentary on the first five books of the Bible, this term "foreigner" implies two types of people who were prohibited from partaking of the Passover: (1) a Jew by birth who has denied God's Law and (2) a non-Jew. Though non-messianic Jews do not recognize it, this foreshadows the Passover's ultimate fulfillment in Christ: physical circumcision and Jewish birth does not guarantee salvation. Salvation, as described below, is a matter of the heart, and made available for both Jews and Gentiles.

CROSS-REFERENCE

Physical circumcision in the Old Testament pointed directly to the "spiritual" circumcision we experience when we receive Christ. Colossians 2:11 describes it this way, "You were also circumcised in him with a circumcision not done with hands, by putting off the body of flesh, in the circumcision of Christ."

CHRIST IN EXODUS

In John 6:53, Jesus pointed to Himself as the ultimate and final Passover lamb -- and the only way to be a part of God's people -- by saying, "Truly I tell you, unless you eat the flesh of the Son of Man and drink his blood, you do not have life in yourselves." Though speaking metaphorically, He was directly pointing His Jewish listeners back to Exodus, where only God's people could partake in the Passover.

DIG DEEPER

In Exodus 12:45, we see that a "temporary resident or hired worker" could not eat the Passover, and there appeared to be no provision for that person to do so.

However, in Exodus 12:48, an "alien" was allowed to observe the Passover as long as he and his household submitted to circumcision. At first glance, it may appear that "temporary resident/hired worker" and "alien" are synonymous, but they are not.

The root word for "alien" includes the concept of "turning," or identifying with the people of God. These non-Jews were ready to cleave unto the God of Israel and turn from their heritage as people formerly cut off from God.

Temporary residents/hired workers, by contrast, made no effort to turn from their heritage to become Jewish, and by extension submit to the God of Israel. Instead, they simply lived in the land with no change of personal, religious, or national identity. God allowed them to stay with His people (see Leviticus 25), but He did not permit them to observe the Passover.

This points to the truth that only those who turn to Christ are allowed to share in the salvation of God's people.

like a native

Have you ever seen a US Citizen oath ceremony? A group of people pledge their loyalty to the United States and renounce previous loyalties. Then, at the end, smiles stretch from ear to ear as they clap and cheer. It's a touching scene.

People from foreign countries routinely visit or even reside in the US without changing their citizenship, however. Especially if they live here for a period of time, it may seem they are the same as one born a US citizen. But there is a clear difference between the temporary resident and a citizen.

God knew when Israel left Egypt, there would be those who would reside among them but who would not change their loyalty, their citizenship, so to speak. Knowing this, He made clear provisions on who could observe the annual Passover meal. Only the Israelites and non-Israelites who had been circumcised could participate. Non-Jews who only temporarily resided with Israel, or those who refused circumcision, could not.

The beauty of this passage is tucked into verse 48. In describing the foreigner who submits to circumcision (and by extension pledges loyalty and worship to God), God says, "he will become like a native of the land." No longer would the foreigner be excluded. He enjoyed full rights of a native-born Israelite.

When we receive Christ, even if we're not native Jews, we become God's people. Most of us understand that. But I believe we might apply this concept further. Could there be something in our "origin" that makes us feel "less-than?"

Perhaps you weren't raised in church and this new world of Christianity seems a little foreign. Maybe you don't have the Bible knowledge your friend has. Or perhaps your past is littered with such dark, secretive sins you don't think you'll ever feel like you're equal to your Christian peers.

That's what is so beautiful about this passage. Regardless of our past, or former idolatry and sin, when we know Christ and accept His sacrifice and freedom, we become "like a native of the land." God sees both His birthed babies and His adopted ones the same.

application

In what areas might you feel like a foreigner in the land? How does this passage whisper truth inside those insecurities?

....

....

....

prayer ~ reflection ~ gratitude

. . . .

. . . .

. . . .

. . . .

to-do today

. . . .

. . . .

. . . .

Week 4 Day 5
Exodus 13:1-16

Observations ~ Main Points ~ Questions ~ Application:

....

....

....

....

....

....

....

HISTORICAL BACKGROUND

Donkeys were unclean animals and could not be sacrificed to the Lord. But lambs and goats, clean animals, could be sacrificed to redeem the firstborn of the donkeys.

IN CONTEXT

All firstborn males were to be given to the Lord as a display of worship and gratitude, since they were the ones spared during the Passover. While firstborn male animals were to be sacrificed, human sons had to be redeemed. This set the Israelites apart from their pagan neighbors, who practiced killing their firstborn children as a sacrifice to their gods.

definition

The word "redemption" in 13:13 means "to bring back to original use." If we liken the "firstborn" to our "first birth" in the flesh as sinners, we see that when Christ redeems us, He brings us back to our original use -- God's original design for us before sin entered the world.

passing down our freedom story

My dad had a rough childhood. The oldest son of an abusive alcoholic father (who was also the son of an abusive alcoholic father), he overcame the statistics and emerged as the only one of his brothers to have never seen the inside of a prison cell.

The first of his family to graduate high school or college, he broke the generational cycle of addiction. As part of his healing as an adult, he began studying alcoholism. When he realized it's a disease, this knowledge not only helped him to forgive his father but also motivated him to share with me our family history and the hereditary nature of addiction.

Growing up, I knew none of that life, but age-appropriately, of course, he shared his horrific stories of abuse with me. He wanted me to know not only where he came from, but also where I came from.

In essence, by passing down his freedom story to me, he attempted to inoculate me from unknowingly walking back into the addiction of our family line.

The account of the tenth plague -- the Passover -- was the beginning of the Israelites' freedom story, and as such, the Lord took great effort to ensure the Israelites passed down this heritage.

But this goes beyond even the exodus. Every minute detail of the Passover pointed directly to Jesus Christ and the freedom He would win for His people. Likewise, our responsibility is the same as the Israelites' charge: pass down your freedom story.

Our children need to know how we came to know Jesus as Savior. But they also need to understand how God frees us from the bondage we may experience after our salvation. Even better, we can share our stories as we live them. Some of the most powerful testimonies I've heard of families are the ones where the adult children can point to when they saw their parent find freedom.

It's not our level of faithfulness, our commitment to the church, our adherence to a high moral code, or even our generous philanthropy that will make the biggest impact on future generations. It's passing on how Jesus freed us from sin and how He continues to free us from bondage

application

How can you make a greater commitment to pass your freedom story onto your children? If you don't have children, this still applies to you. How can you pass your freedom story onto those God has allowed you to influence?

....

....

....

....

....

....

....

> The Lord commanded the people of Israel to proclaim to their children what the Lord had done. It was to be as noticeable as a sign on their hand and a reminder on their foreheads. In the same way, everything we do (hands) and all we desire (heads) should be in accordance with God's word and in response to what He has done for us -- and as noticeable as something in our hands and on our heads.

prayer ~ reflection ~ gratitude

to-do today

Week 5 Day 1
Exodus 13:17-22

Observations ~ Main Points ~ Questions ~ Application:

HISTORICAL BACKGROUND

The shortest route from Egypt to Canaan was the northern route along the Mediterranean Sea. Archaeological digs have shown heavy Egyptian fortifications along this route. Though it might have been shorter and perhaps easier, it would also have plunged the Israelites into Philistine territory. Both the Egyptian and Philistine opposition would have been constant for Israel. Although God could have given them victory, He knew they were too weak in themselves and didn't know and trust Him enough yet to follow Him. (Sidenote: if God had brought them the easiest way, the northern route, they would have never had to cross the Red Sea.)

definition
The glory cloud represented the Shekinah glory of God. It means "to dwell." This glory cloud signified the presence of God with the Israelites.

Joseph said to his brothers, "I am about to die, but God will certainly come to your aid and bring you up from this land to the land he swore to give to Abraham, Isaac, and Jacob." So Joseph made the sons of Israel take an oath: "When God comes to your aid, you are to carry my bones up from here." (Genesis 50:24-25)

CROSS-REFERENCE

Hebrews 11:22 applauds Joseph for his faith that God would rescue Israel from Egypt:

"*By faith Joseph, as he was nearing the end of his life, mentioned the exodus of the Israelites and gave instructions concerning his bones.*"

(See Joseph's exact words in Genesis 50:24-25 in the margin.)

not yet ready for our destiny

I turned the key and locked the office door for the last time. After many tears, I said good-bye to my coworkers and prepared to begin my new life as a stay-at-home mom.

I couldn't have been more thrilled. Leaving my job to be home with my 6-year old son and 2-year-old daughter had been in my heart for over a year, and I felt strongly that home was where I needed to be.

But something kept nagging me. If the Lord wanted me to be home with my children, why didn't I feel that tug when my son was born? We couldn't have made it work financially, having already spent the first five years of our marriage building our lives around two incomes. But even so, the desire never sparked. Not until my daughter began approaching her first birthday did my heart begin to stir.

Around that time, I read Exodus 13:17 and it all made sense. "When Pharaoh let the people go, God did not lead them along the road to the land of the Philistines, even though it was nearby, for God said, 'The people will change their minds and return to Egypt if they face war.'"

Mothering never came easily to me. Back when I struggled with postpartum depression and a colicky infant, I counted the days until I could return to work and recover a semblance of normalcy.

Looking back, I think God saw me the way He saw Israel. My destination was to be at home (like Israel's destination was Canaan), but He knew I couldn't handle it yet. If I had been allowed to stay home earlier, I would have gone back to my Egypt, I'm certain.

Instead, God took me a circuitous route, not unlike the one by which He took the nation of Israel. He needed to draw me nearer to Him, show me His ways, and open my heart to my Canaan.

God knows our weaknesses. He knows the enemies on the shortest path and that we'd choose slavery over war. But in the moment, we struggle with understanding why He seems to take us the opposite direction, deeper into the wilderness.

application

Do you currently feel like God has led you into a wilderness? How does this passage speak to you about God and His plans and provision for you?

....

....

....

....

....

FURTHER APPLICATION

Although God knew the Israelites would turn back to Egypt if they faced war, they left Egypt in "battle formation" (v. 18). Seeing this discrepancy, we understand there is a difference between outward and inward readiness. Sometimes we think we're ready for something but God knows our true capacity. That's when our trust in Him must overshadow our disappointment if He doesn't provide what we expect and when.

prayer ~ reflection ~ gratitude

to-do today

Week 5 Day 2
Exodus 14:1-4

Observations ~ Main Points ~ Questions ~ Application:

CROSS-REFERENCE

Numbers 33:5-8 lists the exact route the Israelites took: Ramses → Succoth → Etham → [turned back to] Pi-hahiroth.

CROSS-REFERENCE

In Acts 16, we see another example of God purposefully leading His men into danger. Acts 16:9 states that Paul received a vision from the Lord to go to Macedonia. In Paul and Silas' first stop, the city of Philippi, they initially saw fruit from their obedience. But they eventually found themselves trapped, beaten, and jailed. In verse 15-34, however, we see the purpose: to share the gospel with the Philippian jailer and subsequently establish a path for the gospel to spread throughout Europe and beyond.

definition

Pi-hahiroth is thought to mean "mouth of the canal" or "mouth of freedom." According to a Jewish scholar, this is the same location as Pithom, the supply city built by Jewish slave labor. Migdol means "tower" or "watchtower."

when God leads us in circles

When my son was in the third grade, we began reading biographies of Christian heroes of the past few centuries. One of my favorites was the story of Gladys Aylward. As a young woman, she felt a strong leading of God to go to China, but her travels there were far from easy.

I thought we'd never get to the point where Gladys would "arrive" at her destination, and even when she did, years passed before she began seeing any fruit from her efforts. At many points in the story, it appeared God was leading her in circles.

At first glance, the initial verses of Exodus 14 seem nondescript. The names of the places God led the Israelites mean nothing to us without context.

Though the exact locations aren't known precisely, it appears God may have led the Israelites in a direction resembling a cursive lowercase "l." It's no wonder Pharaoh concluded the Israelites were confused (v. 3).

God could have led the Israelites straight to the Red Sea, but he didn't. He chose instead to lead Israel in circles, baiting Pharaoh to pursue them.

"Where are we going?" the Israelites must have wondered as the sun appeared on their left one morning and on their right the next.

Don't we often feel the same way? Where is God taking me? Sometimes we feel like we're plodding around in circles in the middle of nowhere.

In an age of knowledge and logic, we must keep in mind that following God doesn't always make logical sense. It may appear to the outside world we're confused, moving in circles.

At the risk of sounding cliché, God always has a plan, and if we're following Him, there's a reason even when He leads us in circles. Sometimes it's not about the destination; it's about the journey.

When it comes to where we are headed, our first question needs to be, "Am I following God?" Sometimes that's the hardest one to answer but it's imperative to do so.

If the answer is yes, then we must trust Him, even if it seems He's leading us in circles.

application

Are you following God in all areas of your life?
__ yes __ no __ not sure

Where do you feel you're wandering and lost, with no sense of direction? How does this text speak into your journey at this moment?

....

....

....

....

....

....

Pray that God will give you the strength to trust Him, even when you can't see where He is leading you.

FURTHER APPLICATION

Search the text today. The answers to the following questions reveal the two purposes God had for leading His people into a trap:

1. So He would receive _____.
2. So the _____ would know that He is the Lord.

What hard situation are you in right now? How could understanding the reason God has allowed this in your life help you see the situation in a different light?

....

....

....

prayer ~ reflection ~ gratitude

to-do today

Week 5 Day 3
Exodus 14:5-14

Observations ~ Main Points ~ Questions ~ Application:

HISTORICAL BACKGROUND

The Egyptian chariots epitomized the scope of Egypt's military power. Comparable to the German Wehrmacht with their superior and terrorizing tanks as they invaded country after country in World War II, the view of chariots struck fear in the hearts of the Israelites.

definition

The word "fled" in verse 5 is used to describe people emigrating to escape a powerful person.

definition

In verse 13, the word "salvation" in Hebrew often took the form of rescue or victory, specifically in military contexts. In a very real sense, their deliverance was fought for and won, just like ours is.

DIG DEEPER

To this point, Israel's attitude was defiant against Pharaoh with no show of fear. Then, in verse 10, they cowered in terror. How quickly their confidence faded, as they could only conceive of two options: death or a return to servitude. Despite all God had done for them, they could not conceive a third option: miraculous deliverance.

no power over you

Blessed to have grown up in a church that esteemed the personal reading of the Bible, I dug into my hardcover New International Version with as much eagerness as a new Christian can possess.

"Read 1 John," I was told, and so I did. But I'll never forget my confusion as I read verses like, "Everyone who remains in him does not sin" (1 John 3:6). Even at ten years old, I knew I still sinned, and as a young believer I didn't understand the passage's broader context.

The book of 1 John and my childhood confusion aside, I think we all may struggle sometimes with understanding exactly what Christ freed us from. We know we still struggle with our flesh, our sinful nature, and idolatrous desires. So besides an eternity with Jesus in heaven, what freedom do we actually possess, if any?

As we approach the pillar event in the book of Exodus -- the crossing of the Red Sea -- we will explore this foreshadowed picture of our salvation. But today, let's look at one phrase to set the stage.

In Exodus 14:13, Moses told the Israelites, "...for the Egyptians you see today, you will never see again."

Because we know the story, we know Moses was predicting the demise of the Egyptian army in the Red Sea, but let's step back a bit and see what this actually tells you and me about our lives.

As we have seen throughout the study, Exodus is filled with "types" -- pictures that point to Christ and our salvation. Egypt represents the world system that opposes people and keeps them in bondage. Pharaoh represents Satan who enslaves people. Israel represents God's people -- individuals who have been delivered from the bondage of the world and of Satan. Moses represents Christ, our deliverer.

So what does this mean for us, when Moses told the people, "the Egyptians you see today, you will never see again?"

Does this mean we will never sin? That we will never long for the things of the world? No.

It means that the power the world and Satan used to have over us no longer holds us captive. We still battle our sinful nature (and we'll get into that more next week), but the power of sin and darkness over us has been broken by our deliverer. They may still influence us, but they are no longer masters over us.

I know that's a lot to take in. But before we can feel it, experience it, live it, we have to know it. We have to understand that the world and the devil have no power or authority over us. Jesus has set us free.

application

Reflect on your life before you knew Jesus as Savior. What did enslavement look like? Even if you received Christ as a child, you can likely look at thought patterns and struggles.

....

....

....

....

....

....

....

Are there areas in your life that you have trouble believing have no power anymore? What are they?

....

....

....

....

....

....

....

....

FURTHER APPLICATION

We see a shift in Moses here. No longer did Moses possess fear and timidity. After seeing God's hand in Egypt, his faith was inspired and he stepped into the role prepared for him. Not so, the Israelites. Moses, having remembered God's past works, trusted Him for the future. Israel only saw the here and now; their fear clouded their perspective and suppressed their faith.

When faced with seemingly hopeless circumstances, do you take after Moses or the Israelites?

....

....

....

prayer ~ reflection ~ gratitude

to-do today

Week 5 Day 4
Exodus 14:15-31

Observations ~ Main Points ~ Questions ~ Application:

CROSS-REFERENCE

One of the Lord's methods of dealing with the Egyptians was to throw them into confusion. He used this tactic in other places in the Bible as well:

- Exodus 23:27 -- God predicted He would throw warring nations into confusion as Israel began occupying the Promised Land.

- Joshua 10:10 -- God made good on His promise and threw Israel's enemies into confusion before them in the Promised Land.

- 1 Samuel 5:9 -- When the Ark of the Covenant (symbolizing God's presence) was in the hands of the Philistines (Israel's enemies), God caused confusion to come down on the Philistines.

- 1 Samuel 7:10 -- God used this same tactic to allow Israel to defeat the Philistines.

CROSS-REFERENCE

Many psalms praise God for what He accomplished at the Red Sea: Psalm 66, 78, 80, 81, 105, 106, and 136

DIG DEEPER

What role did each play in the Israelites' crossing of the Red Sea?

Moses: (14:16) _____

God: (14:17) _____

(14:21) _____

(14:24) _____

The Angel of God: (14:19-20) _____

The Israelites: (14:22) _____

> **definition**
> The "angel of the Lord" in verse 19 is generally recognized as pre-incarnate Jesus.

CHRIST IN EXODUS

Understanding that Moses in this story represents and foreshadows Christ, and the Angel of the Lord is most likely Christ Himself, what conclusions can you draw about Christ's role in our salvation? (Refer to your answers above for help.)

....

....

....

your red sea story

On the edge of our padded theater seats, my family and I eagerly awaited what we were about to see. Lights and sound sought to replicate one of the most well-known events in the Bible, and my adrenaline surged. I willed myself to cast aside my prior mental picture of this Bible story -- ones that started with felt-board characters in my childhood Sunday School classes -- and see the events depicted in the Sight and Sound Theatre's performance of Moses with new eyes.

Only in my adulthood did I begin to understand the significance of this event, that it was more than a one-off miracle of God characterized in colorful children's books. No, the crossing of the Red Sea was more than Israel's history or a sweet bedtime story. It's my story. It's yours.

> If God used the same tactic against future enemies in the Promised Land as He used in defeating Egypt, what does this tell us about His power and tactics over the enemies we encounter as we're living our lives in Christ?

As we studied last week, the Passover symbolized and foreshadowed Christ's death. The crossing of the Red Sea symbolized and foreshadowed His resurrection.

The Passover pointed to Christ's substitution for the penalty of our sins; the crossing of the Red Sea symbolized His power over sin and bringing us into freedom.

Simply put, the Passover and crossing of the Red Sea is a picture of your salvation and mine.

Once we understand this most basic biblical doctrine, we can learn more about our God, our deliverer, and our own salvation. For example, how was Israel saved? By anything they did? Hardly!

Israel was saved by the object of their faith -- God -- not the quality of it.

We, likewise, are saved by the object of our faith -- God -- not the quality of it. Our deliverance comes by the grace of God, not by anything we do to earn God's approval. We can't do anything to earn it; we can't do anything to keep it.

When they exited the Red Sea, Israel's deliverance was final. They never saw the Egyptians again, as prophecy foretold. However, their step onto the other side of the sea was not a step into perfection. Next week, we'll see that they were as messed up and prone to wander as we are. Whether they would choose to walk in the freedom already won for them, well, that is a different story entirely.

application

But for now, take a moment to ponder your own Red Sea story -- your salvation.

Using the deliverance of Israel as a guide, write it out on the next page:

MY EGYPT
What my life looked like before I knew Christ

MY PASSOVER
Circumstances surrounding my realization that I was a sinner and Christ died to pay the penalty of my sin

MY RED SEA
What happened when I accepted Christ's gift of salvation and turned to follow Him

Praise God today for His gift of salvation!

If this exercise is too hard for you and you are uncertain of your story, perhaps you haven't yet accepted Christ's sacrifice for your sins and followed Him into freedom. You can know freedom today, right now, by praying -- and meaning -- something like this:

Lord God, I know that I am a sinner, separated from you. Thank you for sending Jesus to pay the penalty for my sin. I receive your free gift of salvation and follow you today.

Let me encourage you to talk with a trusted Christian friend if you have any doubts or if you prayed to receive Jesus as your Savior and deliverer for the first time. If so, it's important that you know where you go from here.

FURTHER APPLICATION

God's command to Moses seems a little crazy, doesn't it? "Hey, Moses, lift up your hand and part the sea." Sure, no problem. It's reminiscent of Jesus telling His disciples when faced with a hungry multitude and only a lunchbox of food, "you feed them."

When God gives us a command, He fully intends on equipping us for the task. It may seem crazy to us and definitely impossible, but it's those "never could this happen" moments that allow us understand the true power and work of God.

Have you had one of those moments? Or is God asking you to do the impossible right now?

prayer ~ reflection ~ gratitude

to-do today

Week 5 Day 5
Exodus 15:1-21

Observations ~ Main Points ~ Questions ~ Application:

....

....

....

....

....

....

IN CONTEXT

Interestingly, the nations in verses 14-16 were listed in the order Israel would encounter them in the Promised Land:

- Edom (Esau's descendants)
- Moab (Lot's descendants)
- Canaan (Canaan's descendants)

CROSS-REFERENCE

Pausing for praise wasn't a one-time occurrence here for the Israelites. Instead, it set a precedent for future celebrations in Judges 5, Judges 11:34, 1 Samuel 18:6-7, and Jeremiah 31:4

definition

The word for "faithful love" in Exodus 15:13 means loyalty that offers kindness and provision to the needy who have no legal right to assistance.

DIG DEEPER

Nestled in Exodus 15:13 we see the destination of the now-freed Israelites: God's "holy dwelling." God rescued His people so that they would be with Him.

definition

At the end of verse 16, the word translated "purchased" was often used other places to refer to buying a slave. This reiterates that Jesus purchased us from slavery -- a slavery to sin.

pause for praise

He made it! He made it! I'll never forget the day my husband received confirmation that he had passed a critical exam at work. The previous eighteen months of brutal classwork and testing in a simulator as large as my living room all came down to this.

Now, it was time to celebrate.

The problem was, now that he qualified for this next step in his job, he had to look ahead to actually doing it. It was tempting to skip the praise and move forward.

Have you ever had a similar experience? Then you'll probably understand our natural tendency to keep on pushing ahead without pausing to express gratitude.

For all the things the Israelites got wrong, in today's passage, they got something right. After God performed the miraculous, they paused for praise.

Sarah, a friend and Christian blogger, made a statement in an Instagram story one day that resonated with me. She said she takes Sundays off as a modern-day Sabbath so she can focus on remembering what God has done in the past. She said we're so tempted to keep our eyes moving forward that we forget what God has already done for us.

I think we can apply this "pause for praise" in all aspects of our lives, but I think it's even more critical to apply it to our personal salvation stories. Too often we forget what God has done for us, especially if we've known Jesus for any length of time.

> Though two million people experienced God's deliverance that day, each one could say God was "my" salvation (the word my is used five times in Exodus 15:2 alone). No longer did they know the Lord only as the God of their ancestors. He was now their God. As parents and grandparents, may we pray that our children will know God as their own, not only the God of their fathers.

application

Today, let's take a cue from the Israelites, and pause for praise. Read 15:1-21 again and note what you see in the text. Then, spend some time praising God for not only who He was to the Israelites but also who He is to you.

	In Exodus Text:	In My Life:
Characteristics of who God is:		
What He has done:		
Promises He has fulfilled:		
Promises He will fulfill:		

FURTHER APPLICATION

Like Israel, we may forget that our destination isn't a place (or a circumstance, or an answered prayer). It's God Himself and to dwell with Him.

Consider what you see ahead -- the destination in your life that would make everything better (more loving marriage, ideal job, relief from depression, etc.). Contrast that to your true destination:

My destination isn't _____.

My true destination is to dwell with _____ Himself.

prayer ~ reflection ~ gratitude

....
....
....
....
....

to-do today

....
....
....

Week 6 Day 1
Exodus 15:22-26

Observations ~ Main Points ~ Questions ~ Application:

HISTORICAL BACKGROUND

There is presently an oasis in the region that today contains only bitter water. It is believed to be the site of Marah.

CHRIST IN EXODUS

The tree's cleansing effect could represent the cross purifying us from sin. Consider the words "tree" and heal" in 1 Peter 2:24: "He himself bore our sins in his body on the tree, so that, having died to sins, we might live for righteousness. By his wounds you have been healed."

definition

"Grumbled" in 15:24 means "rebellious complaining" and indicates hostility.

DIG DEEPER

Write out the three commands in verse 26 that God gave Israel after their testing:

1. _____

2. _____

3. _____

> **symbols & types**
> Elim represents the spiritual rest and refreshment we receive after accepting Christ's work on the cross.

Look at the progression, at the end of verse 26. If the commands were obeyed, illnesses wouldn't come. Then, God says, "For I am the Lord who heals you." So, why would God reveal Himself as the healer if the illnesses weren't present in the first place? Consider two possibilities.

1. God would heal the people through their obedience.

2. God knew the people would not obey the commands perfectly, so He was prepared to offer healing when/if they sinned again.

Both could be accurate -- for not only the Israelites but for us. As we walk in obedience, we will find healing from the afflictions, wounds, and sin in our hearts. Little by little, with each step in obedience, healing will come. But as fallible people, we won't obey perfectly, so God will continue to be there for us, offering grace and healing as long as we come to Him in repentance.

when you're squeezed

My home environment growing up was about as calm and pleasant as you can imagine. Only once do I recall my parents engaging in a heated argument, and never did I hear them raise their voices -- to one another or to me. The only temper flares I witnessed were at basketball games where my dad, the coach, tossed clipboards and slapped the bench on occasion in frustration.

That's why as an adult, experiencing my own episodic anger confused me. Why would I struggle with my temper when I rarely witnessed it as a child? And why did it only manifest itself once I married and had children of my own?

Though I don't have definitive answers for those questions, I do believe one thing. My struggle with anger has probably always been present. But it never emerged in a notable way until marriage and motherhood squeezed me. They provided the trigger needed to set me off and, in so doing, revealed this ugly trait that had previously remained dormant.

Just like squeezing a sponge reveals the cleanliness (or lack thereof) of the water inside, sometimes it takes outside pressure to show us what lies beneath.

After only three days, the Israelites found they were out of water. Why would God lead them to a place without water? Especially when Elim with its natural springs lay only seven miles away? God tells us why: He led them there to test them. While He knew their inward condition, they did not. They needed to discover their lack of faith and distrust in God's provision, and this would not happen on a road paved with blessing and ease.

The biggest threat to our freedom may not lie in the form of enemies we meet in our Promised Land. Instead, the biggest threat to our freedom may very well lie in our own wretched hearts. And unless we're tested -- squeezed by outside circumstances -- we may very well live in ignorance.

> The biggest threat to our freedom may very well lie in our own wretched hearts.

Because God loves us and has a purpose for our freedom, He can't let us live in ignorance of our sin.

But look at the beauty of this passage. God didn't simply test them, reveal the ugliness, reprimand them, and let that be it. After giving them a plan for going forward, He revealed to them another characteristic of His nature. He's the God who heals.

This healing goes beyond the physical. It's a healing of the heart. And it's not a one-time remedy. It is ongoing.

God knows that, while we are on our journey, we will need continual healing. Yes, we are free children of God, now and always, but the sin in our heart and our nature will continue to afflict us. We will need dose after dose after dose of His healing grace.

When we're squeezed and ugliness comes out, it's hard not to despair at the sight of our decrepit heart condition. But remember we have a God who heals.

application

When was the last time circumstances squeezed you, and ugliness came out?

....

....

....

....

What did that occasion reveal to you about sin in your life and heart?

....

....

....

....

What do you sense God is asking you to do in response? (Ask forgiveness, make amends, etc.)

....

....

....

....

Thank God for being the God who heals you. Pray that you would understand the full depth of this healing.

prayer ~ reflection ~ gratitude

to-do today

Week 6 Day 2
Exodus 15:27 - 16:36

Observations ~ Main Points ~ Questions ~ Application:

IN CONTEXT

Exodus 16:23 is the first mention of a commanded Sabbath rest for God's people. This, of course, would become law in the giving of the Ten Commandments later (Exodus 20:9-11). The Sabbath served as a weekly reminder of their deliverance. Interestingly, while the other nine commandments would be repeated in some form in the New Testament, Gentile Christians would never be commanded to keep the Sabbath as Jews did. The principle of the Sabbath, then, is a rest from work. In the Old Testament, this was literal work, but it pointed to the New Testament's culmination of the concept of any form of [futile] works-based salvation. By celebrating the Lord's Day on Sunday (the day of Jesus's resurrection), Christians celebrate spiritual rest that comes when we accept Jesus' completed work of

definition
Wilderness of Sin is not a euphemism. It's a transliterated Hebrew word that is a shortened form of the word Sinai.

IN CONTEXT

The provision of manna wasn't about the manna itself -- the provision -- it was about pointing to the Provider.

145

Taste and see that the Lord is good. How happy is the person who takes refuge in him! (Psalm 34:8)

CHRIST IN EXODUS

Look at the characteristics of the manna: small, round, white, and sweet. Jesus, as the bread of heaven, fulfilled those characteristics with his humility, perfection, purity, and sweetness. (See Psalm 34:8)

CROSS-REFERENCE

Jesus, in John 6:32-35a, called himself the "bread of heaven," pointing back to manna in the desert.

Jesus said to them, 'Truly I tell you, Moses didn't give you the bread from heaven, but my Father gives you the true bread from heaven. For the bread of God is the one who comes down from heaven and gives life to the world.' Then they said, 'Sir, give us this bread always.' 'I am the bread of life...' (John 6:32-35a)

CROSS-REFERENCE

The grumbling in Exodus 16 didn't stop when God provided manna. Look at Numbers 11:4-8 in the margin to see their continued grumbling after they left Mount Sinai, still longing for the food of Egypt. Similarly, when God meets our needs, do we eventually still want "more?"

DIG DEEPER

Consider other characteristics of the manna from heaven as it relates to Jesus as the true bread of heaven:

• It arrived with the morning dew: The morning dew represents the Holy Spirit, who ministers Christ to our hearts.

• It was always enough: Christ is always enough. He satisfies. He is sufficient.

• It arrived daily: Just as the Israelites needed food for each day, we need Christ and to taste of Him every day.

The riffraff among them had a strong craving for other food. The Israelites wept again and said, "Who will feed us meat? We remember the free fish we ate in Egypt, along with the cucumbers, melons, leeks, onions, and garlic. But now our appetite is gone; there's nothing to look at but this manna!" The manna resembled coriander seed, and its appearance was like that of bdellium. The people walked around and gathered it. They ground it on a pair of grinding stones or crushed it in a mortar, then boiled it in a cooking pot and shaped it into cakes. It tasted like a pastry cooked with the finest oil. (Numbers 11:4-8)

longing for egypt

After years of persuading, my husband finally succeeded in his quest to convince me to buy a camper. Perfectly content with vacations in condos and hotels, I had no fond memories of the few camping trips I had taken in my life. Public bath houses and raccoons invading our cooler? No thank you.

Ultimately, the promise of more travel and the potential for long-lasting memories for our family won me over -- that, and the camper's bathroom, kitchen, living area and bunk beds for the kids. The quaint home on wheels had me ready to hit the road.

In July, after a few test runs, we headed out in excited anticipation for a 13-day excursion to the Western US. Though words can't describe the beauty of Yellowstone, the Grand Tetons, and South Dakota, by about the tenth day, I began to long for home.

> Why would Israel depart from Elim? It seemed like a perfect location. But Elim was the refreshment, not the destination. Sometimes we like where we are and don't want to leave; we forget the blessings we receive are given for our refreshment, but they are not the destination. May we not get comfortable and "settle" in places God leads us temporarily when we know it's not our home.

It's easy to look down our noses at the Israelites in passages like Exodus 16. Only a month after their flight from Egypt and the multiple demonstrations of God's glory and leading, their appetites surged within them.

Regardless of their hope for a new, free existence, the fact remained, they were leaving the most civilized place in the known world for the most barren.

Sure, their previous life held oppression and hardship, but now they faced a foreign nomadic lifestyle with no tangible promise of food or water. They longed for security. Even if Egypt proved hard, at least they knew it -- it was familiar. They knew where they would lay their heads each night and what food would grace their lips.

It's tempting to remember the perks of slavery when freedom proves harder than we expect.

I think that's one reason many new believers in Christ become disillusioned so quickly and fall away. Yes, freedom ushers in joy, and walking with God brings indescribable blessing.

But it's not always easy. Our very natural appetites bubble within us. We long for security, even security in oppression. This new life isn't always easy to navigate. As we come face to face with our own sin and weakness, we begin to long for the former life.

George Morrison put it this way, "It took one night to take Israel out of Egypt but forty years to take Egypt out of Israel."

If there's one concept I want you to come away with this week, it's the understanding that living a life of freedom in Christ -- while joyous and full of blessing -- isn't always easy. We will have battles to fight (as we'll discover tomorrow) and longings to cast aside.

But just as God proved with wayward Israel in Exodus 16, He's always with us. He is our provider. When He doesn't make the road easy or luxurious, it's for a purpose, and we can trust Him. He is guiding us to a Promised Land.

application

In your own life of freedom with Christ, what areas have continued to prove most difficult?

....

....

Describe any longings you've had to "return to Egypt."

....

....

Just as God provided quail and manna for the hungry Israelites, how has God provided for you in your journey, especially when your soul or body hungered?

....

....

FURTHER APPLICATION

The Lord trained the Israelites through the multiple instances of hardship and testing God brought upon them. He knew the enemies they would face ahead. Through these hard times He proved His provision and character and that He could be trusted. They would have to trust Him in much bigger ways in the future.

In what areas have you sensed God "training" you for bigger battles?

....

....

....

prayer ~ reflection ~ gratitude

to-do today

Week 6 Day 3
Exodus 17:1-7

Observations ~ Main Points ~ Questions ~ Application:

CHRIST IN EXODUS

The "rock" in verse 6 foreshadows Jesus Christ. Paul explained it in 1 Corinthians 10:1-6 and most specifically in verse 4: "[The Israelites all] drank the same spiritual drink. For they drank from the spiritual rock, and that rock was Christ." The water that flowed from the rock represented the Holy Spirit being given at Pentecost. Jesus Himself spoke of this in John 7:37-39:

> On the last and most important day of the festival, Jesus stood up and cried out, "If anyone is thirsty, let him come to me and drink. The one who believes in me, as the Scripture has said, will have streams of living water flow from deep within him." He said this about the Spirit. Those who believed in Jesus were going to receive the Spirit, for the Spirit had not yet been given because Jesus had not yet been glorified.
> (John 7:37-39)

CROSS-REFERENCE

The word translated "complained" in verse 2 is not the same we saw in Exodus 15:24. This word, instead, was one used in disputes, often of a legal matter, signaling an escalation in the Israelites' complaints from a grumbling to an outright conflict with Moses. Consider other uses of this same word:

"When men quarrel and one strikes the other with a stone or his fist..." (Exodus 21:18)

"Then Jacob became incensed and brought charges against Laban..." (Genesis 31:36)

DIG DEEPER

In verse 2, Moses asked the Israelites, "Why are you testing the Lord?" This word "test" is the same word God used in Exodus 15:25 and Exodus 16:4, where God "tested" the Israelites. The word "test" can also mean to "prove." God used this testing in the wilderness to show the Israelites their hearts and what they lacked, but here, in verses 2 and 7, the Israelites attempted to test the Lord, to make Him prove Himself. Their testing of God actually showed their lack of faith, and God later commanded them in Deuteronomy 6:16 never to do this.

distrust and complaint

I live in the South, where all the memes are true: college football is the god of Saturdays in the fall. Like any good southerner, I root for my state's team like the rest (woo pig sooie!), but there is one thing about the college football culture that always brings me dismay.

When our team doesn't meet our expectations, the armchair quarterbacks (and more accurately, armchair head coaches) lift their voices in a predictable cacophony. "Get rid of him!"

I always cringe. The daughter of a coach, my heart bleeds for the target of the bellowed criticism. Though no coach is perfect, the masses don't always realize the unseen factors at work in a competitive sport. Still, the ammunition on their tongue aims and fires.

Not much has changed since Moses' time. Life was hard, no doubt. The Israelites followed God from place to place, but when things didn't go as expected, their grumbling grew into hostile complaint. (Not unlike many Facebook posts I see at the end of another disappointing football season.)

> The bondage of resentment will keep us from moving forward in freedom.

It's easy to snub our noses at the Israelites. It wasn't that long ago, after all, that God provided water at Marah and manna in the wilderness. You'd think they would have learned to trust Him by now.

This time, however, their complaints rose not against God per se but against Moses himself. Even Moses, usually patient and quick to defend God's people, grew exasperated and fearful for his life.

Again, I'm afraid not much has changed, college football rants aside. Isn't it easy for us, when circumstances don't turn out the way we had envisioned, to blame our leaders?

We're not getting "fed" at church, so we blame the pastor. Our kids don't like Sunday School, so we don't make them go. We don't agree with decisions made within the church, so we withhold our tithe. Our child struggles in a class so we complain to or about the teacher.

I could go on because this type of disrespect of our leaders is blatant in our culture and sadly it can be found in our faith communities just as often. But if we look deeper, beyond our complaints about the leaders in these situations, many times we will find the heart of the issue has nothing to do with our leaders.

For the Israelites, as for us, the heart of the matter could be found in the people's trust in God. When we fully trust in God, we put our hope in Him, not in the ability of our leaders. Our earthly leaders never will get it right every time. But if our expectations are out of alignment, and we respond in quarreling like the Israelites did, we will find ourselves stuck. The bondage of our resentment will keep us from moving forward in freedom.

But when our trust is in God, we can live securely, trusting that even if God leads us to a place with no water, He will provide.

application

Is there a situation right now where you are struggling with a leader or leadership?

....

....

....

....

Prayerfully ask God what the heart of the matter could be. Could it be a lack of trust in God in a particular area?

....

....

....

How does God want you to respond to what you read in today's text?

- Confess and ask forgiveness from another?
- Take a step toward reconciliation?
- Repent of gossip?
- A renewed commitment to support your leaders?

....

....

....

prayer ~ reflection ~ gratitude

to-do today

Week 6 Day 4
Exodus 17:8-16

Observations ~ Main Points ~ Questions ~ Application:

....

....

....

....

....

....

HISTORICAL BACKGROUND

The Amalekites descended from Esau, the firstborn of Isaac who forfeited his birthright to his brother Jacob. (As a reminder, the people of Israel were descendants of Jacob.)

The nation of Amalek was unlike the other nations Israel fought against in the Promised Land. They were a persistent enemy of Israel who constantly harassed them wherever they went. They were ruthless and brutal, attacking the weak and kidnapping women and children.

CROSS-REFERENCE

In the book of Deuteronomy, in which Moses gave final instructions to the Israelites before they were to enter the Promised Land, he said,

"Remember what the Amalekites did to you on the journey after you left Egypt. They met you along the way and attacked all your stragglers from behind when you were tired and weary. They did not fear God," (Deuteronomy 25:17-18).

CROSS-REFERENCE

Moses gave these instructions to Joshua regarding Amalek before Israel was to enter the Promised Land: "When the Lord your God gives you rest from all the enemies around you in the land the Lord your God is giving you to possess as an inheritance, blot out the memory of Amalek under heaven. Do not forget," (Deuteronomy 25:19). Years later when Saul reigned as Israel's first king, God reminded Saul of what the Amalekites did and instructed him to kill each and every one of them. Saul did not obey completely and was hence rejected by God as king (See 1 Samuel 15 for the account). Later, some Amalekites who likely escaped Saul's failed mission, raided an encampment in Israel and kidnapped the women and children, including future king David's wives and children. David responded swiftly and he and his men defeated the Amalekites (see 1 Samuel 30 and 2 Samuel 8:11-12). Thus, what the first king (Saul) had failed to do, God's second king (David) completed.

not what I signed up for

In the days following September 11, 2001, I worked hard to resume life as it was before the world, as I knew it, changed. A senior in college, I willed my mind to focus on my classes, but even in those classes, it seemed to be all my classmates and I could talk about.

I'll never forget a young man in my bowling class (I had to get that last half-credit of physical education). I'm sure this stocky freshman with the slick blond hair must have played linebacker on his high school football team. But beneath the strut, I saw tenderness, and I'll never forget the fear in his eyes.

He had signed up for the National Guard like many young men do, but now with the looming threat of war, he realized what exactly he signed up for.

symbols & types

Amalek represents the evil, corrupt nature of man -- our sinful nature, our flesh. Just like Amalek opposed Israel on their pilgrim journey, our flesh opposes us on our spiritual journey in freedom. Other ways Amalek parallels our flesh:

• Amalek only came into the picture after Moses struck the rock and the waters flowed at Massah and Meribah (Exodus 17:7). Since this represented Christ's death, resurrection, and the giving of the Holy Spirit, we can understand that our battles with our flesh will only come into the picture after the Holy Spirit is given to us at salvation. Before salvation, we are slaves to sin and there lies no conflict between our flesh and our captor, for they are allies. After salvation, however, the Spirit inside us wars against our flesh (See Galatians 5:17).

• Just as Amalek warred with Israel for many generations, so our flesh will continue to be at war with the Spirit inside us. Our flesh will only be subdued when we are delivered from it at our physical death.

• During the battle with Amalek, Aaron and Hur upheld Moses' arms, an avenue through which the battle was won. These two men represent the two means of triumph we have at our disposal when we war against our flesh -- prayer and the Word.

Before 9/11, my generation hadn't known war. Although volunteering for military service carries the assumption of the possibility, my young friend realized this possibility could become a reality.

When we receive Jesus' beautiful gift of salvation and take our first steps into the glorious freedom He gives, I doubt that we truly understand we've signed up for war.

Though God predicted there would be enemies to conquer within the boundaries of the Promised Land itself, I'm sure Israel was as shocked as my young friend when Amalek attacked.

As you'll see in today's commentary, Amalek wasn't an ordinary nation. They represented something we all face in our Christian lives -- our sinful nature, our flesh.

In Galatians 5:17, Paul writes these words to Christians, "For the flesh desires what is against the Spirit, and the Spirit desires what is against the flesh; these are opposed to each other...."

> For the flesh desires what is against the Spirit, and the Spirit desires what is against the flesh; these are opposed to each other, so that you don't do what you want. (Galatians 5:17)

We hear quite a bit in Christian culture about spiritual battles with the Enemy (Satan and his forces), but I'm afraid we hear far too little about the enemy in our own hearts that, in my life anyway, causes a much deeper threat to freedom.

James puts it this way, "But each person is tempted when he is drawn away and enticed by his own evil desire," (James 1:14).

Let me give you some good news. Our battles with our own Amalek are normal. This side of eternity, they will continue. Why is that good news? Because when we know what the enemy is, we are more equipped to address it. And we're more likely to gear up in the battle rather than run away thinking this Christian life isn't what we signed up for.

More good news: The more we battle our flesh and overcome, the easier the battles become. Just like an adept soldier gains tactical advantage and skill the more he fights, the more we will learn to recognize the enemy, call on our training (the Bible), and rely on our Intercessor in prayer.

Take heart, my friend. You're not alone. Your Amalek will look different than mine. But keep fighting the good fight.

application

Let's get creative. Whether in words or in a picture, write (on the lines below) or draw (in the circle to the right) an avatar of your Amalek. What areas of your flesh do you battle the most? (Some examples: a critical spirit, selfishness, fear, indulgence)

WEAPONS (BIBLE VERSES) TO FIGHT MY AMALEK:

We can't battle without weapons, and one of the most useful is an armory of Bible verses. For each element of your avatar, write down Bible verses you will meditate on and memorize. This may not happen in one sitting, so bookmark this page to come back to it when you see a verse you can use in your battle against your flesh.

prayer ~ reflection ~ gratitude

to-do today

Week 6 Day 5
Exodus 18:1 - 19:3a

Observations ~ Main Points ~ Questions ~ Application:

HISTORICAL BACKGROUND

It is uncertain what Jethro was actually a priest of but most likely he was not a follower of the Lord before this text. Scholars also debate on whether Jethro converted to God or whether he just accepted God as one of many.

CROSS-REFERENCE

Read Numbers 11 for an account where God specifically led Moses to organize the leadership of Israel in a way comparable to what Jethro suggested. Compare the differences and similarities.

destination: God

Perched in the front passenger seat, I unfolded the huge paper about a hundred times. You know what I'm talking about: a real-life map. My dad wanted to make sure we were headed in the right direction on our vacation, and it was my job to find out.

The problem was, though we knew our destination; we did not know our current position. In those pre-GPS days, more than once we stopped for directions, despite having a map in-hand.

Looking back on the Israelites' journey to this point, Moses knew the destination. God had told him at the burning bush, "When you bring the people out of Egypt, you will all worship God at this mountain," (Exodus 3:12). But the path to the destination turned out to be full of more curves and bumps in the road than he had anticipated.

Now, at the foot of the mountain, Moses saw the culmination of God's promise. What cause for rejoicing!

> Your ultimate destination is your relationship with God Himself.

But here's the interesting thing. Although God brought Moses and the Israelites to Mount Sinai, Mount Sinai wasn't their final destination. So why bring them there? As we saw earlier, the quickest the path to the Promised Land did not lead through Sinai.

God knew the people. He knew their hearts, their lack of faith, their roots in Egypt -- He knew it all. He also knew their greatest need -- Himself. At Mount Sinai, God would reveal Himself to Moses and the people and give them the Law that would govern their nation. He would slowly begin painting a picture of their ultimate Deliverer, one brushstroke at a time.

Yes, the Promised Land was the place of the ultimate destination -- the place of the promise. But the ultimate destination was a relationship with God Himself.

The Promised Land represents the victorious Christian life, but like the Israelites, we can be saved by the blood but still get lost in the wilderness of unbelief. That's where Sinai comes in. We gain the strength and tools to take and live in the Promised Land by the relationship with God we develop at Sinai.

application

As we come to a close on this study, I'd like you to spend some time reflecting on what we've gone through these last six weeks. As you answer these questions, feel free to flip back to your answers.

What areas of bondage has God revealed to you in this study?

....

....

....

....

....

....

....

What steps have you taken to address those areas?

....

....

....

....

....

Are there any areas in which you need to continue to respond in obedience?

....

....

....

....

Understanding that living in unfettered freedom in Christ is your Promised Land, how will you commit from this day to draw nearer to Him?

....

....

....

Prayerfully ask God which part of the Bible He wants you to read next. Write it below:

....

....

prayer ~ reflection ~ gratitude

....

....

....

....

....

....

....

to-do today

....

....

....

continue your journey...
Be inspired by real stories of women who have found freedom from various areas of bondage in the Journey to Freedom podcast!

journeywithjill.net/freedompodcast

also by Jill McSheehy...

journeywithjill.net/shop

references

Feiler, B. (2001). Walking through the Bible: a journey by land through the five books of Moses. New York. HarperCollins.

MacDonald, W. (1989). Believer's Bible Commentary. Thomas Nelson.

Scherman, N. (1998). The Chumash. Brooklyn. Mesorah Publications, Ltd.

Walvoord, J. & Zuck, R. (1989). The Bible Knowledge Commentary Old Testament. SP Publications.

Walton, J. (2000). The IVP Bible Background Commentary Old Testament. Downers Grove. InterVarsity Press.

Wiersbe, W. (1998). Be Delivered. Colorado Springs. David C. Cook.